THE LIVING HUMAN DOCUMENT

From The Desk Of
Judy Doll

THE LIVING HUMAN DOCUMENT

Re-Visioning Pastoral Counseling in a Hermeneutical Mode

CHARLES V. GERKIN

Abingdon Press
Nashville

THE LIVING HUMAN DOCUMENT

Copyright © 1984 by Abingdon Press

Fourth Printing 1991

This book is printed on recycled, acid-free paper.

GERKIN, CHARLES V., 1922–
   The living human document.
   ISBN 0-687-22372-5
   1. Pastoral counseling. 2. Hermeneutics. I. Title.
BV4012.2.G474   1984
253.5   83-14972

MANUFACTURED IN THE UNITED STATES OF AMERICA

For Mary
Partner and Companion
in the Story of
My Life

ACKNOWLEDGMENTS

One cannot write a book without friends and supporters who are willing to listen to ideas, react and critique, and, most of all, encourage. In the writing of this book I have been most fortunate to live in the midst of a lively community of scholarship in which the exchange of ideas within and across disciplines is both encouraged and practiced vigorously. I am therefore indebted to a number of colleagues who have read all or parts of what is here presented in one or more of its several revisions. Most particularly I am grateful to William Mallard, E. Brooks Holifield, David Pacini, Walter Lowe, Roberta Chestnut, James W. Fowler, Romney Moseley, and James T. Laney for their careful reading of various chapters and their very helpful suggestions at a number of points. Above all, I am deeply appreciative to Rodney J. Hunter, my close colleague in the teaching of pastoral care and pastoral theology, for his patient and sustaining effort to help me bring my ideas to clarity of expression. A number of my students have also been helpful in numerous ways: Richard Osmer, with whom I first worked through the unfamiliar literature of philosophical hermeneutics; Gary Myers, whose clinical interests and expertise provided a common set of pastoral counseling practice concerns with me that nourished the effort; Emma Friedman-Morris and David Galloway, whose reactions to some of the early beginnings of the book encouraged me to persist.

I am also deeply indebted to a great number of persons who over the years have trusted me with the deep issues of their lives in relationships of pastoral counseling. From them I have learned at levels that go beneath simply the sharing of ideas. Some of them appear in these pages in the concrete vignettes of my clinical work.

Their names and other identifying data have, of course, been changed to protect the sacred privacy of their lives, but they are indeed real people whose courage to face and work through the truths about themselves that counseling evoked has caused me to count them among my most valued benefactors.

CONTENTS

Pastoral Counseling in Transition

How can pastoral counseling be at the same time both an authentically theological and a scientifically psychological discipline? This is the root question facing the pastoral care and counseling movement with increasing urgency in the present state of its development. Since that movement surfaced in the 1940s and 1950s as a major adaptation of the American church to the twentieth-century cultural situation, its primary identification as a pastoral or psychological discipline has been the subject of considerable discussion both in the burgeoning literature the movement has produced and in the clinical centers where pastoral counselors are trained.

We have now entered a time of transition with regard to the issue of the primary identity of pastoral counseling. Through the first four decades of the modern period in pastoral care and counseling, psychological and psychotherapeutic concerns have unquestionably been dominant. This was true in part because much, if not most, of the new knowledge that gave rise to the resurgence of pastoral care as an emphasis in ministry was psychological knowledge. Not only that, the neo-orthodox period in theology took a strong swing away from primary concern for human religious experience toward a more objectivist preoccupation with the "otherness" of God and human dependence upon God's transcendent action. Pastors with primary concern for their ministry to persons undergoing the common problems and crises of everyday life were quite naturally drawn to the new language and potentially helpful techniques coming from the psychologists. Pastors with counseling interests found that they were not alone in their concern for suffering, troubled persons. Psychiatric physicians, psychologists, social workers, marriage and family therapists, and a whole host of others in what have come to be called the helping professions, were bringing other identifying images and language traditions to the task of alleviating human psychic and spiritual suffering. Some of these other helpers—physicians, for example—had historic roots as deep as those of Christian ministry. Others had more recently emerged in the pragmatic bustle of twentieth-century secularization with its human effort to take charge of the conditions of human life and solve human problems.

Meanwhile broad and deep shifts in the cultural paradigms of Western society were taking place. As the language of theology became more centered on its own history and tradition, all around the new languages of psychology and the social sciences were more and more deeply permeating American cultural life. Human experience in America was becoming psychologized. As Philip Rieff so pointedly stated, the therapeutic paradigm was becoming triumphant over other language paradigms as the primary mode for consideration of human individual and relationship problems.[1] This deep cultural shift toward the primacy of psychological and psychotherapeutic language had the effect of granting considerable social authority to the psychological experts who spoke that language with fluency and precision. Pastoral counselors, if they were to be recognized as persons with expertise in human problems, were in subtle but powerful ways confronted with the necessity of evidencing fluency with psychological language, though in most situations their authority also remained linked to the traditional authority of the pastoral office.

A second effect of the cultural shift toward a psychological language paradigm took place at another level of popular culture. Psychological self-help books appeared by the dozens on bookstore shelves. Popular psychologies abounded as, one by one, various simplified versions of more complex theories were introduced for popular consumption. Pastors generally, and pastoral counselors in particular, were expected by their parishioners and invited by their secular psychotherapeutic colleagues to become not only acquainted with, but proficient in, the application of these popular remedies for the miseries of twentieth-century life now seen as fundamentally psychological rather than religious. In short, pastors and pastoral counselors were caught up in the movement of a social process that permeated every nook and cranny of American life.

If one reads the theoretical literature of pastoral care during the decades of this reformative period, evidence of both the power of the therapeutic movement and of an increasing tension between theological and psychological language as formative for pastoral counseling is easily apparent. Most of the acknowledged "big names" in pastoral counseling theory—Seward Hiltner, Wayne Oates, Paul Johnson, Carroll A. Wise, and later Howard Clinebell—give some attention to the primacy of theology and the ministerial tradition in forming the basic stance of pastoral counselors toward their task. All these theorists seek carefully for congruencies between pastoral care considered with psychological paradigms in mind and pastoral care seen from a biblical or traditional theological perspective. Theological and biblical warrants are developed for the quality and structure of counseling ministry that a more psychological understanding of the pastoral situation seems to demand. Thus a certain rough correlation emerges between theological-biblical and psychological-psychotherapeutic considerations.

It is beyond the scope of this book to attempt to trace out all the interplay between biblical and theological themes, on the one hand, and psychological themes, on the other, in the pastoral care literature of the last four or five decades.[2] Rather, my purpose is more limited. I wish simply to locate myself and this book in relation to the various options that have been emerging. In that regard it is important to differentiate somewhat between the written texts produced by leaders in the field and the more amorphous but rich and equally direction-shaping process going on in the clinical centers among the practitioners and clinical teachers of pastoral counseling and clinical pastoral education.

In the writings of the last thirty years several options have been proposed, each associated with one or two of the "big names." Seward Hiltner, whose early book, *Pastoral Counseling*,[3] set the standard for pastoral counseling through the decade of the fifties, has consistently sustained a dialogue among Freudian (and, more particularly, neo-Freudian) psychoanalytic thought, a modified Rogerian methodology for counseling, Reformed theology, and Whiteheadian process thought. Hiltner's growing ambivalence concerning the pastoral counseling movement's efforts at professionalization and involvement with psychotherapeutics led him in the years since the publication of his *Preface to Pastoral Theology*[4] to concern himself more with issues of general ministry and the development of a pastoral theology emerging from pastoral operations in the parish than with pastoral counseling as such. The outcomes of Hiltner's legacy for those who value his contribution are that the placing of pastoral counseling within the contexts of the church and a general theory of ministry must be taken very seriously and that the posssibilities of theological dialogue with psychology via the vehicle of process thought is opened up.

Wayne Oates, steeped in the warm biblical piety of Southern Baptist culture, has been, of course, more attracted theologically to the vocabulary of neo-orthodoxy. This is particularly true of his two books written in the early sixties, *Christ and Selfhood* and *Protestant Pastoral Counseling*.[5] Oates' pastoral counseling theory thus evidences much less interest in detailed appropriation of psychotherapeutic technique. Rather there is a more general sense of awareness of nuances of dynamic relationships and of changing styles of psychotherapeutic fashion within a deeper and more consistent concern for the formation of the pastor's counseling ministry coming from historic Christian sources. As late as 1974, Oates wrote:

> I return to my earlier theme: the pastoral counselor is not an eclecticist picking and choosing from this, that and the other system of therapy. Nor is he a methodological purist who sells out his sense of history and buys into one particular kind of therapy. The pastoral counselor has both a short memory and a long memory. He has a clear knowledge of the history of the interaction of pastoral counseling with changing emphases in psychotherapy. This is a short memory. He has a long memory of history also in that he is constantly correlating the wisdom of the Hebrew-Christian tradition with what he hears and sees going on among psychotherapists and their patients.[6]

Carroll A. Wise and Paul E. Johnson, both of whom were educated and found their theological home in the personalist theologies of Borden P. Bowne and Edgar S. Brightman, drew their early counseling theoretical framework largely from Rogerian theories.[7] Johnson was strongly influenced by the interpersonalism of such psychologists as Harry Stack Sullivan, whereas Wise from early in his career was more attracted to psychoanalytic dynamic theories. The theological personalism of both Wise and Johnson permitted them to lodge the integrative task relative to theology and psychology largely in the person of the pastor and the interpersonal relationship between the pastor and the suffering person. The extent to which this is the case is made quite explicit in Wise's magnum opus published nearly thirty years after his first book on counseling methodology.[8] By this time Wise had decided to abandon the term pastoral counseling in favor of the term that had become more and more popular with the counseling practitioners during the 1970s: pastoral psychotherapy.

Although Wise acknowledges the fact that the word "psychotherapy" has in popular usage been taken over by the various secular psychotherapeutic guilds, he stakes a pastoral claim for its usage by pastors on the basis of the New Testament usage of the terms "psyche" and "therapia" or "therapuo."[9] In Wise's modern usage, however, the word psychotherapy takes on enough of the technical psychotherapeutic meaning that one cannot help wondering as to the practical difference between pastoral psychotherapy and any other kind of psychotherapy. That difference, Wise proposes, can only be sorted out in the personal experience of the pastor. It is a function of the pastor's personhood.

> This dual orientation (theological and psychological) is not always comfortable. The abstractions of theology and psychology are not easily reconciled, nor should they be. They stem from completely different faith assumptions; they involve different dimensions of being; and they have their own ways of creating and resolving tensions. Furthermore, specific dynamic processes within the personality of the pastor, such as guilt feelings, come into conflict with theological and psychological ideas in a manner that cannot be resolved by reason alone. One side or the other then may be denied, or the pastor may vacillate from one to the other.
>
> The resolution of this situation must come in the person of the pastor. This must involve his emotions and strivings, as well as his intellect. Such resolution usually requires emotional growth, moving to levels of being. . . . This requires a commitment to the process of being and becoming, to internal discovery rather than to the integration of diverse theories.[10]

In a sense, this commitment of the process of integration to the personhood of the pastor stems both from Wise's personalist theology and his heavy involvement in psychotherapeutics. It therefore "works" for him in ways that become much more problematic for the pastor who embraces another theological orientation. Furthermore, the implied disdain Wise exhibits for the hard intellectual work of analysis and critique of the various psychotherapeutic psychologies with the tools provided by the theological and philosophical traditions leaves pastoral counseling as a discipline vulnerable to the hazards of too easy smoothing over of fundamental issues of truth and purpose. The person as pastoral counselor is left too much on his or her own without the corporate discipline and supportive boundary setting that rigorous attention to theoretical issues provides. Minus that level of rigor the movement is in danger of becoming flaccid and undisciplined.

Howard Clinebell, whose book *Basic Types of Pastoral Counseling*[11] became a standard text after its publication in 1966, marked the break of the movement from virtually unanimous allegiance to Carl Rogers' methods and opened the way to an increasing eclecticism in relation to therapeutic methodologies. The door was opened to a period of intensified faddism and embrace of popular psychologies in the pastoral care movement. Clinebell's writings, while giving some attention to theological models of ministry, do not give evidence of serious probing of theological questions and issues. Rather, "growth" in psychological terms is loosely associated with "liberation" as a theological catchall.

In the clinical centers that multiplied by the dozens during the decades of pastoral counseling's rapid growth, a process of discussion and growing tension among psychological options and between theological and psychological paradigms parallel to that in the literature was taking place. In the ferment of increasingly successful collaboration with representatives of the psychologically oriented disciplines in the mental health field, clinical pastoral education flourished, as did the practice of pastoral counseling. Orienting fledgling ministers to psychological perspectives on grief, illness, interpersonal conflict, and family relationships was exciting and rewarding work. The style and ethos of clinical education for ministry strongly supported the model of integration made explicit by Carroll Wise and Paul Johnson. The person of the pastoral care trainee became the focus of attention. Did the pastor in his or her person evidence the integration of biblical and theological images of ministry with psychological savvy and expertise? This became the central training issue.

Important and necessary as the focus on personhood has been in the training of the pastoral counselor, it has in profound ways turned the pastoral care movement in a therapeutic direction. Practitioners of the pastoral arts, particularly practitioners newly introduced to the craft and still exploring the depths of their own history and selfhood in the virtually standard ritual of personal psychotherapy, are prone to adopt psychological language. As one of my theological friends has said, theological reflection can in that situation become like the bumper sticker slapped on the bus as it is pulling out of the parking lot on its way to a psychologically determined destination. Despite these natural hazards of the clinical situation, however, concern for theological rootage and biblical warrants for pastoral decision and action have persisted, indeed in the current rising cultural disaffection with psychology, have become often voiced passionate matters of interest.

Two other important voices have come forth with increasing strength and conviction during the decade of the seventies: concern for the corporate process of care in the community of faith and the revolt against modern consciousness, including its psychological paradigm, a concern to which I have already alluded. The first voice will be heard more in the background than the foreground of what is contained in these pages. That is not because the concern that pastoral care be seen as a larger activity than the one-to-one relationships of the pastor is not important. Unquestionably it is. No direction offers more promise for the years just ahead than does this recovery of the meaning of community, of corporate care and its relationship to liturgy, worship, and the recovery of context. But if the time of transition the pastoral care and counseling movement is now in is to have an outcome that relates just these concerns to the most profound and critical of human suffering and conflict, attention must also be given to the transitions called for in pastoral *counseling* as done by the professional pastor and pastoral counseling specialist. It is to this more narrow but related concern that this book is directed.

The second concern for the recovery of pastoral counseling's theological roots is currently being voiced from all sides. From some have come strongly worded demands for a return to classical modes of pastoral care and ancient theological constructions. This latter concern has been most polemically voiced by Thomas Oden who, after having made important contributions to the literature of the psychology-theology dialogue through his earlier writings,[12] has issued a clarion call for a return to the classics, both in pastoral care and in theology.

> The task that lies ahead is the development of a post-modern, post-Freudian, neo-classical approach to Christian pastoral care which has taken seriously the resources of modernity, but which has also penetrated its illusions, and having found the best of modern psychotherapies still problematic, has turned again to the classical tradition for its bearings, yet without disavowing what it has learned from modern clinical experience.[13]

In the primary thrust of this terse paragraph, Oden has set forth the central task for pastoral care and counseling in a new time of transition. It is first a task of recovery of a genuinely theological definition of the task of pastoral care and counseling. Such a theological definition must penetrate the actual practice of the counseling task deeply enough to include methodology. That means that theological language must find its way into the reflections of the pastoral counselor on the concrete decisions of the counseling process. In appropriate ways theological language must likewise find its way into the actual conversation of a pastoral counseling relationship. The theological hermeneutic must take its place at the very least alongside the psychological hermeneutic and at crucial times even assert its authority as primary for pastoral counseling.

The task of this time of transition is not simply, however, that of recovery of theological origins and theological language.[14] We are twentieth-century persons who must make use of twentieth-century tools. The rich resources of psychological diagnostics, and psychological interpretations of developmental process and its consequences in human behavior in the present, as well as the limits it places on the possibilities for change in the future—all these tools for analysis and interpretation must be brought to bear on the pastoral task. But Oden is right in a fundamental sense. Our bearings in a time of transition must indeed come from a reappropriation of Christian language—what in theological circles is often called fundamental (not fundamentalist!) theology.

Here comes into view an understanding of the task at hand which will be developed in this book. Somewhere in the gap between the personalistic emphasis of Carroll Wise and Paul Johnson, together with their clinical counterparts in the recent clinical pastoral tradition, on the one hand, and the clarion call for a return to classical theological language sounded by Thomas Oden and others, on the other, lies another alternative. We will call that alternative a hermeneutical theory of pastoral counseling.

The word "hermeneutic," or "hermeneutical," is, of course, a complex word with a long and complicated history of usage.[15] In its broadest meaning it has to do with the art and science of interpretation. The original image from which the Greek word sprang came from the wing-footed messenger god, Hermes, who was associated with the "function of transmuting what is beyond human understanding into a form that human intelligence can grasp."[16] Within that broad definition, a hermeneutical perspective sees all human language systems, including both theology and psychology, as efforts to penetrate the mystery of what is beyond human understanding and make sense of it. The common mysteries of concern to both theology and psychology are, of course, human experience and behavior. Building on very different paradigmatic images of the core truths of human reality, each language world develops a vocabulary of words and imagerial forms by which these mysteries are to be interpreted, understood, and, where possible, explained.

A hermeneutical theory will therefore come at the task of relating two language worlds, such as those of theology and psychology, to a specific human function, such as that of pastoral counseling, by first acknowledging the discrete boundaries of each world. Languages cannot easily or deftly be interchanged. Each comes at the interpretive task with a different set of formative images. Just as German and English or French and Swahili can only be to a limited degree translated back and forth across cultural and language barriers, so the languages of psychology and of theology remain discrete and point to different meaning worlds.

We will be utilizing the general interpretive theory of hermeneutics at other levels along with that of the general problem of relating psychology and theology, however. We will also be exploring the possibilities that come into view when the life of the self, be that the self of the person seeking help or of the pastoral helper, is seen as fundamentally a process of interpretation.

From very early in life, even as early as infancy, the developing self is presented with the necessity of making interpretations of what is experienced. Even before there is language this is the case. The "story" of an individual life begins with the earliest experience of being a self separate from other selves. Drawing upon the images and language of culture as transmitted by parents and other significant figures, the self slowly develops a myth or story by which all experience is interpreted. From that mythic story new experience is anticipated and given meaning. Thus a notion of the self as hermeneut and myth maker—interpreter of experience— will be explicated. As we shall see, these individual interpretive myths tend to mix freely the images and languages of "public" or corporate stories about the way things are and the more private images of self and world that emerge from concrete experiences of the self. Interpretive mythic stories act as vessels within which both symbolic meanings and affect, both positive and negative, are held together.

A hermeneutical theory also provides an approach to understanding the problem of the uniqueness of pastoral counseling that is helpful in a number of ways in this time of transition. Pastoral counseling will be here seen as a process of interpretation and reinterpretation of human experience within the framework of a primary orientation toward the Christian mode of interpretation in dialogue with contemporary psychological modes of interpretation. The most basic tools of pastoral counseling are therefore seen as hermeneutical tools—the tools of interpretation. The pastoral counselor works self-consciously as a representative of Christian forms of interpretation rooted in the primordial images of Christian understanding of the world. But the pastoral counselor, just because of his or her Christian orientation, comes at the interpretive task with profound respect for and hospitality toward the particularity of the experience of the individual sufferer. To represent the Christian mythos is not heavy-handedly to impose it. The hermeneutical philosophical tradition will be seen as offering ways of visualizing the encounter between the pastoral counselor as representative of Christian interpretation and the sufferer as interpreter of self experience that elucidates some of the nuances of that encounter across the boundaries of language and experience worlds.

One way to envision what we are attempting in proposing a hermeneutical theory of pastoral counseling is to see the proposal as an alternative to what has come to be called pastoral psychotherapy. As practiced by its practitioners, pastoral psychotherapy in its methodology has come to rest its primary work of decision making and action on psychological and psychotherapeutic criteria. The extent to which the fundamental images of Christian language are active in methodological decisions has become muted or idiosyncratic to a particular pastoral counselor. A fresh effort at even-handed usage of both psychological and theological paradigms is needed. That effort can be facilitated by viewing both languages from a hermeneutical perspective. Each provides a hermeneutic, a way of seeing and interpreting the phenomena at hand, and thereby each illuminates or brings forth something that remains hidden when seen from the other perspective.

If a theory of pastoral counseling is to function at the level of methodology, it must sooner or later come to grips with the problem of change. What is it that the pastoral counselor as helper hopes to change in the person seeking help? How is that change to be brought about? Psychotherapeutic theories themselves vary greatly in their responses to these questions. How is the pastoral counselor to view these problems? Does a theological perspective alter or give peculiar shape to one's responses to these questions? I shall argue that it does in significant ways, affecting both the expectations of the pastor and actual decisions and behavior in the counseling context.

In proposing a hermeneutical theory of pastoral counseling it is not my intention to state a polemic or call for a time of repentance from the movement's involvement with psychotherapeutics. Much has been gained by ministry generally and pastoral care ministry in particular from the years of conversation with the mental health movement. Pastoral counselors need to continue to be psychologically minded enough to incorporate the insights coming from secular psychotherapy.

But I am concerned to offer an alternative to the absorption of pastoral counseling ministry into psychotherapy to the point of loss of the pastor's rootage in the Christian tradition and language. A disciplined way must be found to preserve that rootage while yet remaining open to other hermeneutical perspectives. That task cannot be left simply to the person of the counselor. I wish to point a direction and outline a possibility for the development of such a discipline. Some readers may find an affinity between this proposal and the earlier work of Wayne Oates. Like Oates, I am concerned that the pastoral counselor develop both a long and a short memory. Like Oates, I am profoundly desirous that pastoral counseling preserve its Christian orientation. That means, at the very least, preservation of a Christian vocabulary.

Because the theory I am proposing has taken form over some years of direct involvement in pastoral counseling practice and teaching in both clinical and academic institutions, I shall begin with a short interpretive sketch of the story of my life experience that has brought me to this proposal. It is not an uncommon story, at least not as pastoral counselors' stories go. It simply tells of the chain of events and experiences that produced a way of seeing and interpreting what pastoral counseling is about. The extent to which the story and the evolving theory it produced are generalizable or convincing will depend upon the possibilities for moving ahead in a time of transition they provide. For, you see, the primary function a hermeneutical interpretation should serve is to open a way ahead. It is when the way ahead is cloudy that the hermeneutical question needs to be asked.

Hermeneutics and the Life of the Self

Life Story
and the Story of
an Emerging Theory

It is probably true that books, like sermons, are all in some sense autobiographical. Whether the book be a novel or a technical, academic text, it will reveal themes and images that are of importance to the author, themes and images that have gathered about them the contents of the author's experience. Books are interpretations of life.

At one level what follows on these pages is an interpretation of my life as a pastoral counselor. Some years of experience in that role in a variety of contexts have produced themes and images around which that experience has clustered, giving that experience interpretation and meaning. Writing about these themes and images is an effort to share how one pastoral counselor thinks about what he has been doing.

The importance of this way of stating the purpose and structure of the book needs perhaps to be underlined. In a crucial sense practice preceded reflection; experience came before interpretation. For me (and I suspect for the majority of pastoral counselors) practice, the experience of being a pastoral counselor, did not take place as the clear and careful application of theory about it. Theory did not come first and fulfill itself in its application to practice. The experience, at least as it is now remembered, came first. In clinical context, parish and hospital, in church and home, office and counseling room, I was thrust into the experience of being a pastor and a pastoral counselor. Reflection and theorizing came later. To be sure, I had some images in my head as I began to practice the role, but they were ill-defined and vague images. Some came from things I had heard in seminary; the more basic ones came probably from what I had unconsciously observed and incorporated from my minister father. But in a fundamental sense, the experience of being in the role came first; reflection and theorizing came later. Thus the description of what follows as an interpretation of the life of a pastoral counselor seems important. A theory and, I would hope, a theology of pastoral counseling may emerge from the interpretive reflection. But it will be a theory and a theology that only provide some images and themes that may prove useful to others who reflect on their experience. It will not be a theory and theology that can be readily applied as an a priori to experience.

The Pastoral Counselor as Listener to Stories

Pastoral counselors are, more than anything else, listeners to and interpreters of stories. Persons seek out a pastoral counselor because they need someone to listen to their story. Most often the story is tangled; it involves themes, plot, and counterplots. The story itself is, of course, an interpretation of experience. To seek counseling usually means that the interpretation has become painful, the emotions evoked by the interpretation powerful and conflicted. The search is for a listener who is an expert at interpretation, one who can make sense out of what has threatened to become senseless, one whose interpretation of the story can reduce the pain and make the powerful feelings more manageable. To seek counseling sometimes means to seek an ally who will confirm one's own interpretation of experience as over against another interpretation insisted upon by another person whose interpretations carry weight with the seeker. For these and other complex reasons the one seeking counseling comes asking for a fresh interpretation of what has been experienced, a new "story" for his or her life.

The stories persons bring to the pastoral counselor are most often told in very ordinary language, the language of relationships to mother and father, sister and brother, children and neighbors, occasionally of relationship to God. The images and symbols that are used to tell the story come from the particular familial, cultural, and religious milieu of the person. The interpretive stories make use of (more accurately, are embedded in) a language world that the teller of the story takes for granted. That language world provides images, symbols, evaluative words, and word vessels for feelings that the storyteller uses to construct an interpretation of the raw stuff of experience. Indeed, for humans, it is impossible to separate experience from language.

If the pastoral counselor comes from the same language world as the teller of the story, he or she will likewise take these same meanings for granted. Anyone who has ever attempted to counsel with a person from a radically different cultural background than one's own, such as an Oriental (assuming the counselor is a Westerner), will know quickly how dependent we are on taken-for-granted meanings and images.

But if the pastoral counselor is a good listener to stories, he or she will soon recognize that there are subtle differences in the way individuals within the same cultural milieu make use of language symbols and images. Private meanings that come from private interpretive experience permeate the telling of the story. So the pastoral counselor soon learns that he or she is living on the boundary, "looking over the fence," as it were, catching glimpses of the meanings, images, symbols, and mythic themes by which the other person is interpreting his or her experience. To listen to stories with an effort to understand means to listen first as a stranger who does not yet fully know the language, the nuanced meanings of the other as his or her story is being told. Needless to say, one of the first lessons of life on the boundary is that it is important to avoid, at all costs, the temptation to stereotype or take for granted.

The Pastoral Counselor as a Bearer of Stories

The pastoral counselor is not only a listener to stories; he or she is also a bearer of stories and a story. The pastoral counselor does not come empty-handed to the task of understanding the other's story and offering the possibility of a new interpretation. The pastoral counselor brings his or her own interpretation of life experience with its use of both commonly held symbols, images, and themes from the cultural milieu of the counselor, and the private, nuanced meanings that have been shaped by the pastoral counselor's own life experience and its private interpretation. Not only that, the pastoral counselor brings to the task whatever he or she has collected from the images, concepts, theories, and methodologies of the disciplines that undergird pastoral counseling—theology, psychology, communications or systems theory, and the like. As a representative of the discipline of pastoral counseling, the counselor has stood and continues to stand on the boundaries that separate these language worlds, each of which offers its own interpretation of the human situation and condition. From all this experience of life on boundaries between language worlds, the pastoral counselor brings to his or her task a veritable storehouse of images, interpretive notions, and connections between meaning and the data of experience. The art of pastoral counseling is in large part the art of drawing upon that imagerial storehouse in the formation of a response to the heard story of the one seeking help. That process, when joined with the process of hearing accurately the story of the other as one having a language and integrity of its own, opens the way to a dialogical encounter from which a new and more hopeful interpretive story for the other's experience may emerge.

Pastoral counseling may thus be understood as a dialogical hermeneutical process involving the counselor and counselee in communication across the boundaries of language worlds. The dialogue takes place at many levels, some between the counselor and counselee, still more within the counselor as he or she sorts through the images, themes, and symbols of the various disciplines that have been appropriated in a search for those that seem apropos or make meaning sense out of what is being heard. The interpretations that result must then be related to the one seeking help in ways that enable that person to restructure his or her experience. A new set of images emerges that structures a new, less painful and more hopeful story. The old raw experience, now gathered into new image meaning vessels and integrated with new experience provided by the counseling relationship, takes on new meaning and a way ahead is opened.

My Pastoral Counseling Story

Since the notion of pastoral counseling as hermeneutical dialogue may come as a strange and new one to the reader, it may be helpful for me to spell out in some detail the story of my pastoral counseling pilgrimage, which led toward the formulation and claiming of this image. Not all the details can be shared; that would be too lengthy and unnecessarily personal. The bare outline of the story will, however, be useful in giving the reader a sense of the process by which the concept came to have importance for me. Remember that, like all stories, this one involves and is itself an interpretation. My hope and expectation is that in sharing it I may make connection with the reader's story. It may in fact in certain ways be typical of the stories of members of my generation of pastoral counselors.

My father was a teller of stories. The stories he told were mostly of people he had known through his ministry as a circuit preacher beginning in the 1890s. He later served small town-and-country churches in the Midwest, moving frequently from place to place as the itinerant system to which he belonged required. His conversations with people, which as a small boy I often overheard, were much of the time made up of stories to which he listened and stories he told in response. I cannot rightly recall ever overhearing him engaging in a theological conversation with a member of his congregation, nor do I remember any such discussions with his fellow pastors, with whom he loved to converse at great length. But I remember stories, and most often stories with a point related to the follies and foibles of people, their good and bad morals, their successes and failures. His sermons were more overtly and directly theological, though they too were filled with anecdotes and moralistic stories. Thus I grew up hearing stories—stories about people.

The story about my ambivalent decision to follow my father into the ministry need not be told here except to note that it came late in college after earlier premedical studies that were academically relatively successful but personally dissatisfying. I remember a profound desire to work with people in relation to the real issues of living. That led me to an academic interest in psychology and sociology. My college academic work did not take me into religious studies at all, except for one very important directed study with a favorite professor who introduced me to William James and the other psychologists of religion of the late nineteenth and early twentieth centuries.

Seminary brought me into my first encounter with the serious study of theology, biblical studies, and church history. The content of the courses I found interesting, but, as with my earlier study of the hard sciences, somehow personally dissatisfying. Biblical studies, then preoccupied with the historical dating of materials and authentication of text fragments, seemed removed from my vague, but definite, desire to be with people. Theological language seemed abstract and therefore unable to speak clearly to the problems of my own living as an adolescent becoming adult and my beginning efforts at ministry. My psychological interests would not have found a home at the seminary (there was not yet a department of pastoral care!) except that I happened to take a course offered one term in the evening by Fred Keuther, then secretary of the Chicago group in the old Council for Clinical Training of Theological Students in the United States and Canada. Fred talked about people and their problems of living. He also talked about psychoanalysis and its new way of probing for the hidden causes of human problems. Keuther had been one of the first students of Anton Boisen, the founder of what was then called clinical pastoral training. Boisen came to one session of the class. I thought him a strange man with his twisted face, penetrating eyes, and thumping cane. But I was attracted to what he said about the study of "living human documents" and mental illness as a sickness of the soul analogous to fever in the body.

I decided to go to Elgin State Hospital for a quarter of clinical training midway in my seminary studies. Boisen was not my supervisor for that experience. He had recently retired and had been replaced by William Andrew, though Boisen still had an office at the hospital and was very much present in the program. Bill Andrew had recently completed seminary, had been trained as a clinical training supervisor, and was now deep into psychoanalysis. We read English and Pearson's *Emotional Problems of Living*[1] and Otto Fenichel's *The Psychoanalytic Theory of Neurosis*.[2] Theologically speaking, we talked at length of God's unconditional love and the human desire for freedom from compulsion, psychological and moralistic. These concepts later became linked in my mind with Carl Rogers' "unconditional positive regard"[3] and Erich Fromm's contrast between the authoritarian and humanistic conscience.[4] Seminary and some graduate study of counseling and guidance completed, I accepted an appointment back in my Methodist home conference in Topeka, Kansas, a major reason for the choice being that I would be near the by then famous Menninger Foundation. I had vague hopes of pursuing further my interest in clinical training and psychoanalysis, the latter because I had by now become convinced that the darker mysteries of my own and others' lives could best be probed while prone on the analyst's couch! My first sermon as a frightened but excited young neonate pastor was titled, "As a Man Thinketh in His Heart." Both goals (clinical pastoral training and psychoanalysis) were later achieved, and I became a clinical pastoral supervisor, duly certified (we called it accredited then) by the Council for Clinical Training.

It should be obvious from this outline of my life story during the years of my entrance to the ministry that a primary hermeneutical image that was at work in my self-understanding as well as my formation of a nascent theory of pastoral ministry was drawn from psychoanalysis understood, in the apt phrase of Herbert Fingarette, as "the search for the hidden reality."[5] The true motivations of persons which produce conflicts and suffering were seen as largely hidden, not only buried in the unconscious residue of childhood familial experience, but hidden in the highly symbolic meaning of their actions and relationships. The language world of psychoanalysis held the keys to unlocking those hidden realities. Insofar as there was any genuine use of theological language, the symbols tended to be filled with psychological content. The way I liked to think of the problems of those two language worlds, which seemed to speak in very different ways about the struggles of the human spirit, was to say that psychoanalytic psychology spelled out in infinite detail what theology had generalized about in its concepts of sin and estrangement, brokenness and alienation. Questions concerning the meaning of redemption and salvation were a bit less easily transposed into the psychoanalytic hermeneutic, but somehow they were symbolically related to the therapeutic process in which I was involved and toward which I attempted to direct my relationships as pastor and clinical supervisor.

Pursuit of the psychoanalytic hermeneutic of suspicion of the presenting surface and the search for the hidden reality did not, however, remove me from concern with religion. Rather it revealed to me both the depth of my own religious nature and quest and enlivened my awareness of the profundity of the central religious questions: ultimate meaning, the human need for an "Other" beyond parents and significant human others, and the question of death. These three revelations came into focus for me one day when I was flooded with an awareness of the recurring religious symbols that appeared in my dreams and associations and awareness of the personal significance to me of my father's death seven years prior to beginning the psychoanalysis. A deeper and more compelling connection between religion and experience was kindled and a previously dormant interest in theological language was awakened. Discovery of Paul Tillich's writings provided the avenue for pursuit of those interests.

Professionally, during the fifties and sixties, the more I became involved in both interdisciplinary clinical experience through a pioneering effort to work with delinquent youth, crisis ministry in a large urban medical center, and later a program of alcoholism treatment, as well as in my own pastoral counseling practice, the more the question of pastoral counseling's unique perspective on the human condition became a question for me. Many of my colleagues in the pastoral counseling movement, though they gave token homage to theology, seemed increasingly to be living, thinking, and working out of psychological or psychotherapeutic presuppositions. Pastoral counseling ministry and psychotherapy were becoming synonymous. The psychotherapeutic hermeneutic was becoming the organizing image for ministry in this specialized field. Some had moved from the psychoanalytic hermeneutic of suspicion to other therapeutic models informed by a hermeneutic of growth and actualization of human potential. But theology in any substantive sense remained in the background. With these trends I was thoroughly uncomfortable.

Meanwhile, I was slowly becoming aware of a growing body of literature that represented the beginnings of a critical reconsideration of the "psychologizing" of human experience by Western culture. Philip Rieff's *Triumph of the Therapeutic*[6] was an important book for me in that regard, as was Erich Fromm's *Heart of Man: Its Genius for Good and Evil*.[7] At the same time, the collapse of neo-orthodoxy in some theological circles, climaxing in the short-lived but powerful death of God movement, called me into a deeper intellectual consideration of the fundamental questions of faith and its viability in a scientific-technological age. An invitation to present a paper on the topic "Human Suffering and Divine Consolation" for a graduate seminar in a university religious studies program proved crucial because of its demand that I share explicitly theological reflections on my clinical experience with human suffering. That paper underwent several revisions over a period of years and finally emerged in print as a portion of the chapter entitled "Suicide, Hopelessness, and Despair" in *Crisis Experience in Modern Life*.

By 1970 I found myself back in a theological seminary, this time invited to relate my interest in "clinical theology," the appearance of theological questions in concrete experience, to the formation of young novices in ministry. It was also an invitation to enter into the kind of day-to-day dialogue with theologians and biblical scholars that I had been experiencing previously with physicians, psychologists, and others in the helping professions. Meanwhile, my clinical practice of pastoral counseling continued to feed my growing concern for a more even-handed interdisciplinary approach to reflection on that practice which did not subordinate theology to psychotherapeutic theory or subsume psychotherapeutic language into a heavy-handed insistence on the authority of theological word usage and God talk.

It was at this point of convergence of all these movements in my life as a pastoral counselor and teacher of ministry that I began the serious work on my earlier book, *Crisis Experience in Modern Life*. In that book I attempted to examine some paradigmatic experiences of individual and family life crisis from a broad interdisciplinary perspective. Theologically, the book developed into an examination of the problems presented by the loss of a deep and powerful sense of the providence of God in much of modern life. Accompanying that problem was the practical pastoral theological problem as to how a sense of God's activity on human behalf could be restored. The problem became, in the work that emerged from the writing of that book, a hermeneutical one. Persons in crisis were seen as caught between a hermeneutic of despair and a hermeneutic of hope and expectation. Much of the problem of crisis experience was seen as a loss of the sense of continuity, with the accompanying difficulty in moving into the open-ended future with hope and faith.

Since the writing of the crisis experience book, its hermeneutical themes have continued to occupy my attention. The notion that any way of coming at the problem of understanding what the world and human life are about is built upon certain primordial images from which all subsequent constructions of ideas and attitudes flow is to me a fascinating notion. Applied to the Judeo-Christian tradition that simple hermeneutical notion allows one to catch a glimpse of the profundity of the implications of the core image of the Creator God who relates to creation with faithfulness and to human beings as to children. That image gave origin to a whole way of seeing everything that is. It provides a hermeneutical key for understanding and making sense of everyday reality, of human relationships, and of existence itself. It also shapes the most basic questions that we who live in that tradition ask about what occurs in our experience.

Modern psychologies, of course, tend to have at their core very different paradigmatic images, though these images also have their historical roots, some of them in the history of Christian thought. Some psychologies have a biological core, as, for example, the notion of primitive biological drives that is central to classical Freudian theory. Others have a central organizing image of the self as subject in process of development and adaptation to the world of relationships. As we shall see, one of the interesting developments in psychoanalytic psychology in recent years has been the controversy over the intermixing of these two paradigms by such theorists as Heinz Kohut and certain of the object relations psychologists.

The hermeneutical perspective has come to have for me both very practical and analytical-theoretical value. It provides a means for sorting out the ways in which the pastoral counselor can make judgments concerning both the appropriate use of psychological theories and tools and the points at which a theological perspective most appropriately asserts itself in pastoral counseling practice. But even beyond that, the hermeneutical perspective has become for me a way of seeing the life of the self or, in more Christian terms, the life of the soul. That life is first and fundamentally a life of interpretation of experience. It is in the joining of event of experience and interpretive meaning that the life of the soul takes place. More about that later!

In the Introduction I made brief reference to the problem of change, what it is that changes, and how change is brought about, as a difficult and crucial question for all psychotherapy as well as for pastoral counseling. That problem will in a number of ways provide an organizing theme for the next three chapters, as well as for later chapters that deal more specifically with pastoral counseling methodology. Readers are encouraged to follow that problem as a kind of red thread running through both the theological and the psychological materials with which we will be working. It is around the theme of the question of change that the differences between a theological and a psychological perspective become most clear. But it is also around that theme that the two perspectives most usefully supplement each other. The change theme likewise provides the arena in which a hermeneutical theory of pastoral counseling becomes most useful and illuminating.

The connection between the ideas and the theories to be discussed in the pages to follow and my own life as a pastoral counselor in a variety of settings may not always be readily apparent. My desire to contribute to a general theory for pastoral care and counseling dictates a degree of objectivity and distance. But the reader should be assured or warned, as the case may be, that the concepts and images set forth in the next and subsequent chapters are those that have clustered over time around my own life on the border of language worlds as a pastoral counselor. They are ideas that emerge from praxis. I will try to make the connections between ideas and lived experience in the role explicit at points through case material and reflection on my own practice. I will also try, insofar as seems useful, to explicate the connections between the most important ideas and the historical and academic traditions from which they come. This latter task seems to me particularly crucial in a time when pastoral counseling as a discipline must establish its own mature identity among the practical disciplines of ministry and secular healing. But the organizing principle that will determine the ideas to be developed as well as the manner in which they are developed will be that of sharing what has been illuminating and enriching for my reflection on my own practice. Thus the living human document I hope to disclose is in a fundamental sense my own. With that in mind, it seems fitting that we now turn to the task of developing a hermeneutical explication of the paradigmatic image of the living human document.

The Living Human Document: Boisen's Image as Paradigm

When Anton Boisen first suggested that pastors should include in their preparation "the study of living human documents," he proposed an analogy the implications of which have never been fully developed. Boisen is generally considered the founder of clinical pastoral education in America and thereby one of the progenitors of the twentieth-century pastoral counseling movement. His concern, however, was only secondarily with pastoral counseling as such. More basic was Boisen's concern that the objectifications of theological language not lose touch in the minds of pastors with the concrete data of human experience. His fear was that the language of theology was being learned by seminarians and pastors without that connection being made. Only the careful and systematic study of the lives of persons struggling with the issues of the spiritual life in the concreteness of their relationships could, in Boisen's view, restore that connection. For Boisen this meant the study of "living human documents."[1]

By his assigning of priority to the study of concrete religious experience Boisen discloses his ties to the psychology of religion tradition shaped in the late nineteenth and early twentieth centuries by William James, Edwin Starbuck, James Leuba, G. Stanley Hall, and others. The pragmatism of that tradition is evident in the primacy Boisen gives to the question as to how religious experience functions to give shape to the encounters of individuals with problems of living. Boisen was, however, concerned with more than simply the study of religious experience. His research interest was accompanied by a passionate concern for the welfare of troubled souls. Though I do not recall ever hearing him use the term "pastoral counseling," clearly the pastoral activity that has come to be called by that name was not only of concern to him, but had for him profound religious meaning. In his later years he was, in fact, highly critical of the involvement of his followers in psychoanalysis and secular psychotherapy. For Boisen the cure of souls had to do fundamentally with the raw stuff of religious experience.

Parenthetically, a word about my own reaction to Boisen's critique of psychotherapy at the time I first heard it is worth noting. To a young seminarian then experiencing the excitement of the newly discovered language of psychotherapy as both liberating from the stereotypical moralism of the Midwestern conventional piety on which I had been reared and concrete in its attention to the hidden dynamics of behavior, Boisen's criticism seemed narrow and confining. Viewed from the vantage point of later historical developments and my own self pilgrimage as a pastoral counselor, his perspective makes more sense.

Anton Boisen's image of the human person as a "document" to be read and interpreted in a manner analogous to the interpretation of a historical text has, up to the present, simply been taken as an admonition to begin with the experience of persons in the development of ministry theory. That certainly was central to Boisen's intention. Boisen, however, meant more than that. He meant that the depth experience of persons in the struggles of their mental and spiritual life demanded the same respect as do the historic texts from which the foundations of our Judeo-Christian faith tradition are drawn. Each individual living human document has an integrity of his or her own that calls for understanding and interpretation, not categorization and stereo-typing. Just as the preacher should not look to proof texts to be twisted into the meaning sought for, so also the individual human text demanded a hearing on its own merit. Furthermore, Boisen was wary of most of the attempts current at the time of his work to "explain" or assign specific organic or developmental causation to the phenomena exhibited by the troubled souls he studied. Rather he thought of them as persons whose inner world had become disorganized so that that world had lost its foundations.[2] Boisen therefore wanted to take the language and the gestures of the troubled person with utmost seriousness as language and gesture that could be interpreted, understood, and given response as one would the language of a textual document. To the living human document he assigned the same authority and right to speak on its own terms as hermeneutical scholarship had learned to assign to the historical text, be that a New Testament text or any other written record of human experience left by a writer of another time and place. Boisen claimed that right for his own experience and his interpretation of it.[3] The troubled person's own reporting of his or her inner world of experience was to be respected and heard as having an authenticity and right of its own, no matter how peculiar its language. What was needed was an interpreter and guide.

As one who claims Anton Boisen as a spiritual ancestor, I have found myself in recent years more and more drawn to and intrigued by this central organizing image of Boisen's work as opening a possible avenue of reflection whereby some of the problems of the enterprise he helped spawn may today be considered. Does the image of the person who is the object of our pastoral care and counseling as a living human document open to us a possible way of approaching the task of restoring pastoral counseling to a sense of its mission and purpose defined theologically? Can that image and its implications help us rebuild the connections between what we as pastoral counselors do and say with persons in our ministering work and the language of the historic texts that have shaped our theological heritage?

It is common knowledge that pastoral counseling, as it has emerged in the late twentieth century, has built most of its operationally primary modes of reflection upon its work out of the images and concepts, the presuppositions and ontological assumptions of the psychological and behavioral sciences. So much has this been the case that the danger exists that the life-giving connection between historic Christian faith and pastoral counseling practice could be broken.[4] Insofar as that becomes the case, the perceptual and conceptual world, the world of meaning, in which the pastoral counselor does his or her work becomes a world no longer inhabited by the representations of faith and salvation, sin and redemption. Rather one finds oneself looking for and seeing a world peopled by persons afflicted with neurotic symptoms, identity conflicts, and compensatory behavior—all good and useful word images, to be sure, but images largely sterilized of religious meaning.

Language constructs world. To have a world, to live in a world, means, for humans, to inhabit a time and place in which a certain language is connected with experience to give meaning to that experience. More than anything else, the capacity to make meaning marks the human as human. Whenever any event occurs in our lives, be that so small an event as stubbing one's toe on a crack in the sidewalk, or so "large" and significant an event as entering into a marriage or contracting a dread disease, it does not become an experience to us until language is attached to the event and it is given meaning. As a matter of fact, because we live in worlds constructed by language, the connection of language and event is an automatic process. Reflection may create new meanings, but the immediate connection of words to experience happens quite unselfconsciously.

To speak of the person as a living human document is to acknowledge this connection between life and language. It is to acknowledge that to understand what Boisen calls the inner world is dependent upon understanding the language by which that inner world of experience is connected to external events. To understand the inner world of another is therefore a task of interpretation—interpretation of a world of experience that is itself an interpretation of the myriad events and relationships that make up a life. Said another way, the task of understanding another in the depth of that other's inner world is a hermeneutical task. It is therefore subject to all the problems and possibilities that the interpretation of an ancient document, such as a New Testament Gospel or Epistle, involves. The difference is that this document is living and continues to disclose itself in new language and behavior that expresses its inner world.

Approaching the literature of the philosophical tradition that has come to be known as hermeneutics with this concern in mind, one is immediately struck with some interesting parallels between Boisen's work and that of several of the nineteenth-century pioneers in the hermeneutical tradition, most notably Friedrich Schleiermacher and Wilhelm Dilthey. In both Schleiermacher and Dilthey we find the same profound respect for the integrity of subjectivity—the particularity and authority of the lived experience of the individual which defies the possibility of reductive explanation.

Friedrich Schleiermacher, the great nineteenth-century German theologian generally considered to be one of the fathers of hermeneutics, developed what he called a general theory of hermeneutics designed to be applicable to every language statement, oral and written. He directed his attention first to ordinary conversation in which there is a shared language available to both speaker and hearer. This constitutes a "universal element" to which general rules and conventions apply. Both speaker and hearer stand under the power and structure that have shaped that language world. But there is also a personal message or "particular element" to be transmitted. To hear this message requires something more than simply a technical knowledge of the language in which the message is couched. To discern this particular meaning, Schleiermacher concluded, required another level of interpretation, which he termed "psychological" or "divinatory." This latter process required intuition and imaginative feeling for the one who produced the text or the spoken word.[5]

Anyone who has attempted to understand with empathy the spoken communication of a troubled person will undoubtedly resonate with Schleiermacher's notion of "divination," slippery as that notion may be when we try to define it rigorously. The image the word conveys conforms to the mystery, the puzzlement, and the intuitive risk involved in listening to another person with a view toward grasping the subtlety and nuance of his or her spoken and unspoken communication. I am myself reminded here of the many occasions when, as a mental hospital chaplain, I have found myself trying to decipher, "divine," what a psychotic patient was trying to tell me.

Wilhelm Dilthey, a philosopher and literary historian who lived from 1833 to 1911, took up Schleiermacher's task and found in the discipline of hermeneutics the foundation for all disciplines that interpret expressions of the inner life of humans, whether those be human actions, law, art, or literature.[6] Dilthey, contesting much of the mechanistic imagery of the physical sciences of his day, contended that for study of human phenomena new models of interpretation had to be forged based on categories of "meaning" instead of "power" or "force," as was the case in the natural sciences. "We explain nature; man we must understand," said Dilthey.[7] As in Schleiermacher, for Dilthey to understand means to grasp the mind, or, in Boisen's language, the inner world, of the other person. While understanding involves cognition, it is finally something more than cognitive awareness. It occurs in those moments when life is grasped by life and understanding of shared experience takes place. For Dilthey this meant that all understanding of human experience is fundamentally historical; meaning and meaningfulness are contextual. They emerge from the situation of a time and place.

Interpretation of the meaning of the inner experience of another person likewise is dependent upon the situation in which the interpretation takes place. In this fashion Dilthey's perspective radically questioned the validity of applying the methodology of the hard natural sciences to human subjectivity. Scientific methodology necessarily involves a subject-object mode of interpretation. Human experience, simply because of its historical particularity, requires a different mode of inquiry. To consider any representation of the human experience from the "distance" that the subject-object mode implies, means to lose track of just that historical-contextual particularity that must be respected in regard to human experience.

More recent hermeneutical scholarship has caused Schleiermacher's concept of divination to fall into disrepute precisely because it lends itself to the projection of one's own preconceptions onto a text, as is, of course, the case with "divinations" in pastoral conversations. Dilthey's neat division between understanding of the "human" and explanation of the "natural" has likewise been called into question by the recognition that human meaning and natural processes are always intertwined and interrelated. Dilthey's question concerning the problem of objectification and distance in subject-object modes of inquiry continues to be a lively one in hermeneutical theory. Dilthey recognized that self-understanding itself required a certain distancing on the part of the self from its own introspective subjectivity. Dilthey spoke of the search for self-understanding as involving a kind of hermeneutical detour through reflection on the objectified expressions of others all down through history.[8]

One like myself, who has been steeped in clinical methodology involving the use of verbatim reports of conversations and critical incidents in pastoral relationships, finds a certain resonance and confirmation in Dilthey's notion that self-understanding comes about through the distancing of reflection on objectifications of experience. Not all distancing is therefore a bad thing. By gaining the distance provided by reflection on "objectified" accounts of pastoral encounters, we come more truly to know ourselves as we have functioned in a relationship now seen from a slight distance.

For Dilthey this "hermeneutical detour" necessary for self-understanding gave evidence that we humans are historic beings. Who we are is always embedded in a historical process that gives shape to our lives. We can never view ourselves as from outside our history, for we are who we are in and through our history.[9]

Here we encounter the first hermeneutical problem for the interpreter of the living human document. The pastoral counselor as interpreter, like the reader of the New Testament, does not come empty-handed. He or she comes bearing a history and a language world. More accurately, he or she comes embedded in a personal and social history and immersed in one or more language worlds from which the images, symbols, and meanings are drawn with which to make an interpretation.

If one is to hear truly what the other person has to say in its own integrity, there must be a breaking through of the barrier that stands between the language world of the hearer and that of the speaker. Stated more fundamentally, to "know" another means to enter that person's world in such a way that a merging of experienced reality can take place. The ancient Old Testament image that associates knowing with intercourse between the sexes expresses the truth that an intimate merger or interpretation must take place if one is to truly know another. Theologically speaking we encounter here the primordial sense of incarnation. To know another in the incarnational sense is to enter that other's world and to have the other enter our world. Hermeneutically speaking, this is possible only because of and to the extent that we are able to enter the other's language world, the world of the other's meanings. In the same way, if we are to be known by the other person, the other must in some degree enter our world, the language of meaning which we bring to the encounter. It is right at this point that the language world out of which the pastoral counselor shapes his or her perceptions and response to the other person becomes crucial. If that be a language world inhabited by the images of theology and faith, the counselee will be invited into a world shaped by those images. If that be, on the other hand, a language world shaped by the images of secularity, it is into that world that the counselor invites the one seeking help.

Traditionally in pastoral counseling theory this process has been spoken about in the language of empathy, rapport, and acceptance. To empathize with another is to put oneself in the other's place, to experience the actuality of life as the other experiences it. Anyone who has attempted to relate to another, particularly another who is troubled about his or her life experience, knows how difficult that is to do. Despite all our efforts, our own situation as an "other" to the one to whom we are relating enters into who we are in that situation. Our own perceptual and interpretive capacities come quickly, automatically, into play. The question must indeed be asked as to whether it is possible for us in the fullest sense to abandon our own perceptual and interpretive world in order to empathize with, become one with, the world of another.

Turning again to the hermeneutical tradition for help with this problem, I have been drawn to the thought of another, more contemporary philosopher writing in this tradition, Hans-Georg Gadamer. Like Dilthey before him, Gadamer takes the position that, since one always stands within the flow of historical process, it is erroneous to consider the hermeneutical task in subject-object terms, as if one could stand apart and view the spoken, written, or other artistic expression of another as an object to be examined and analyzed as from an ahistorical position. Rather, Gadamer says, it is much more of a dialogical process in which what is hoped for is what he refers to as a merger or fusion of horizons of meaning and understanding.[10] This means that when we attempt to understand another, whether through a written text, an artistic production, or in a conversation, we take with us into that attempt our prejudices, our "pre-understandings," our biases. They are part and parcel of the world in which we live and experience the other; they make up the horizon of our understanding.

> If a person is trying to understand something, he will not be able to rely from the start on his own chance previous ideas, missing as logically and stubbornly as possible the actual meaning of the text until the latter becomes so persistently audible that it breaks through the imagined understanding of it. Rather, a person trying to understand a text is prepared for it to tell him something. That is why a hermeneutically trained mind must be, from the start, sensitive to the text's newness. But this kind of sensitivity involves neither "neutrality" in the matter of the object nor the extinction of one's self,

but the conscious assimilation of one's own fore-meanings and prejudices. The important thing is to be aware of one's own bias, so that the text may present itself in all its newness and thus be able to assert its own truth against one's own fore-meanings.[11]

The notion of a "horizon of understanding," which we take with us into every new situation we encounter, is an important one for pastoral counseling considered from a hermeneutical perspective at several points. First, it points to the finite limits within which we work in an effort to understand another person. The fulfillment of empathy is revealed as having a horizon, a limit of possibility. Indeed, care itself (as in pastoral care) is disclosed as care within the limit of a horizon, subject to the biases and meanings the pastor takes into the act of care. Care and empathy are therefore shown to be reciprocal human activities in which the subjective limits of carer and one cared for are made vulnerable. Care involves the opening of the horizon of our understanding to admit the intrusion of the world of the other in the hope and expectation that something truly new may be shared in the encounter—a "fusion of horizons" in which the other is permitted to speak, to question our understanding and vice versa. We will later need to explore this idea further theologically in relation to the image of the activity of the Holy Spirit. For now I simply want to take note of an important implication for pastoral counseling of the image of the encounter with the other as opening the possibility for a fusion of horizons of understanding.

Gadamer's image of understanding as involving the intersubjective merger or fusion of horizons of understanding is important for pastoral counseling in a second and equally important sense. It allows pastoral counseling to move beyond the mind-set taken over from the scientific-technological world of most of the secular helping professions. It breaks apart the understanding of pastoral care and counseling as involving primarily the application of learned techniques to the solving of human problems by the pastor. Care and counseling, considered as a hermeneutical process are not expressible in the mode of subject to object, pastor to parishioner, counselor to counselee. Such techniques as are brought by the pastor are rather to be seen as expressions of a formed world of meaning which both invite the one seeking help to share that meaning world and intrude upon the meaning world of the other. Techniques may thus impede as well as or rather than facilitate the disclosure of the "text" of the living human document. In Gadamer's language, the "text" must be allowed to tell the pastor something, to "assert its own truth against one's fore-meanings."

For the pastoral counselor who considers Hans-Georg Gadamer's analysis of intersubjective fusion of horizons of understanding, yet another significant consideration comes to the fore, one that contains both promise and problem. For Gadamer the intersubjective encounter between interpreter and textual or other human expression contains the possibility, indeed the lively necessity, that both interpreter and the object of interpretation be changed at the fundamental level of meaning. To come to know the object of interpretation does not mean to discover its meaning in some static, "the way it really is or was" sense. Rather the fusion of horizons opens up a new and novel vision of possibility, a new and novel opening into what might be.

It is just at this point that the pastoral counselor in search of answers to the most thorny of therapeutic questions, the question of change, may see a glimmer of light. What is it that facilitates change in a counseling relationship? Just what does it mean to change? Why is it that some persons in relation to some pastoral counselors in some circumstances are able to make changes in their way of being persons so that the old problems of life and relationships disappear or are ameliorated? Why is it that some do not, try as the counselor may? What is it that makes change possible?

The studies that have been done concerning therapeutic outcome all tend to locate the factors that make for change in the therapeutic relationship.[12] But precisely what is it in the therapeutic relationship that effects change? Gadamer's hermeneutical concept of the fusion of horizons of understanding may offer a clue. That way of imaging the relationship offers the possibility that it is in the richness, the delicate balance and respect experienced intersubjectively with both counselee and counselor open and vulnerable to the intrusion of the new that some fresh possibility for a changed way of being a person in relation to another and therefore to all others may be opened. The barest outline of an image of merging horizons of two or more persons, each a living human document now opened to interpretation and question by the other, begins to take form as the image of the context in which change is possible.

Gadamer speaks of this process as a kind of game.

> The common agreement that takes place in speaking to others is itself a game. Whenever two persons speak with each other they speak the same language. They themselves, however, in no way know that in speaking it they are playing this language further. Common agreement takes place by virtue of the fact that speech confronts speech but does not remain immobile. In speaking with each other we constantly pass over into the thought world of the other person; we engage him, and he engages us. So we adapt ourselves to each other in a preliminary way until the game of giving and taking—the real dialogue—begins.[13]

The thrust of Gadamer's argument here is that it is in the intersubjective "play" between members of a conversation or any interpretive encounter that something truly new, which transcends what each participant brought to the encounter, emerges. In the play of genuine encounter all participants are changed. I will in a later chapter take this notion and apply it to the interplay of myths of the self brought to the counseling relationship by the one seeking help and the pastoral counselor's representation of the Christian myth. It is in the play and interplay that takes place between these two language horizons of understanding that change in accordance with the Christian myth can take place. Further development of both the concept of myths of the self and the pastor as conversational representative of the Christian myth will need to be carried forward before the promise and possibility of that process will be clarified.

But, as I said earlier, Gadamer's hermeneutical analysis of the interpretive encounter as a fusion of horizons of understanding contains not only a promise but also a problem. Simply stated, the problem it contains lies in its suggestion that change consists simply in altered understanding. If the encounter under consideration is one with a historical text, such as a passage of scripture, that vision of change may seem at first to be sufficient. One's cognitive understanding of a human problem or question may indeed be changed as Gadamer supposes, by the alteration that takes place in the horizon of one's understanding when that text is encountered intersubjectively. One's cognitive understanding of one's human problem and situation may be changed by the intersubjective encounter of a conversation with another. But is that enough? Can such an alteration in one's horizon of understanding really create and sustain change at the level of behavior and affective relationships? Does the image of the self as a living human document finally break down?

Coming to grips with this problem is central to the purpose of this book and will require considerable work in subsequent chapters to this one. But to begin the movement toward a solution that I want to make requires first going back to Boisen's major project, that of understanding the nature of the suffering of the mentally ill and, most particularly, his own suffering. In the letter referred to earlier from the introduction to *The Exploration of the Inner World*, Boisen connects events in the troubled person's life with ideas concerning the nature of things.

> Something had happened which has upset the foundations upon which his ordinary reasoning is based. Death or disappointment or sense of failure may have compelled a reconstruction of the patient's world view from the bottom up, and the mind becomes dominated by the one idea which he is trying to put in its proper place. That, I think, has been my trouble and I think that is the trouble with many others also. [14]

Boisen here places the problem of the troubled person at the point of linkage of events of experience and ideas concerning their meaning. One might say that he locates the problem at a point of blockage or distortion in the process of interpretation of what has occurred in the life of the person.

Here Boisen points to the existential problem and dilemma of life for the human as meaning maker. On the one hand, there is the flow of hard reality in the occurrence of events. From the time we are born we are affected by a whole range of aspects of reality and events over which we individually have little or no control. As finite creatures we are simply subject to these realities and events. They make up what Paul Tillich refers to as our destiny. [15] There is something hard, unyielding, and forceful about that givenness of the human situation—a hard, unyielding force that takes multifarious shapes and forms in the uniqueness of the human situation for any individual.

In the midst of this givenness of our individual situation, each of us must, if we are to live with any integrity at all, somehow on the other hand retain a sense of our own agency, our own ability to do and be someone with power to act and choose. It is at this point that the human capacity to make meaning comes into play. We must exercise our need and capacity to make meaningful interpretations of who we are, what the world is, and what, given our situation, is most meaningful—what Tillich calls our ultimate concern.

When I think of the extent of this human need and capacity to make meaning out of any situation of givens, I always think of the child-beater's child. On more than one occasion I have had the painful opportunity to help such a young person try to make sense out of what has happened to him or her. Again and again I have seen the battered child struggle with the possibility, even certainty, that he or she must have deserved the beating, else it would not have happened. Such is the human insistence on retaining some sense of agency, of participation in whatever hard or unyielding force may be affecting our lives.

So the events and forces in our lives must be linked through language to meaning. Behind that human desire and insistence lies the threat of chaos and absurdity, the ultimate threat to our sense of being human agents. For Boisen, the problem of the deeply troubled person was just at this point. Ideas and meanings could not be fitted together with experience. A "reconstruction . . . from the bottom up" must be undertaken.

Now, if I attempt to relate this to the problem that emerged in our consideration of change in Hans-Georg Gadamer's concept of the fusion of horizons of understanding, the two-sidedness of any analysis of human change presents itself. Objectively speaking, there is the side of change brought about by changing forces that shape and impinge upon human destiny. Placement of the child-beater's child in a foster home with kind and loving foster parents may produce such change. And making of this level of change requires on the part of the helping person or persons an analysis that takes the form of explanation of the forces that are shaping the situation in which the child's experience is embedded.

At this point I am reminded of the discoveries of Freud and the psychoanalytic tradition he founded, which point to the fact that not all "forces" which determine the existential situation of the person are external to the self. There are also "forces" within the self which interplay dynamically to create a certain givenness to the situation of that person at any point in time. Much of Freudian and neo-Freudian theory was developed and continues to be developed for the purpose of describing and explaining these forces.

Paul Ricoeur, the philosopher-theologian whose hermeneutical project has sought to join existentialism, phenomenology, and psychoanalytic theory, speaks in his monumental work on Freud of two levels of language that are intertwined in all of Freud's work.[16] On the one hand, there is the language of force: the economic, hydraulic, dynamic metaphor that is built upon a presupposition that all human behavior is determined by a confluence of forces. On the other hand, there is the language of meaning, of interpretation of symbols and symbolic acts that relate human desire and intention to culture. Ricoeur seeks in his study of Freud to unite these two seemingly contradictory languages in what he refers to as a "semantics of desire."[17] Consciousness, Ricoeur says, is for Freud not a given in human life. Rather it is a task—a task related to the epigenetic necessity of gradually leaving behind infancy and childhood and becoming a mature and autonomous adult. For Freud, however, the adult remains subject to his or her childhood and the "givens" that childhood contained, left behind as a kind of unconscious residue.[18]

The above brief summary fails to do justice to Ricoeur's complex and multilayered interpretation of the Freudian project, but it is perhaps sufficient to suggest an avenue of approach to the problem confronted in the appropriation of Hans-Georg Gadamer's intersubjective understanding of the change of the self's horizon of understanding. The possibility is presented that the horizon of understanding consciously brought by the person seeking help to the therapeutic encounter contains, to use Ricoeur's terms, both a language of force and a language of meaning. The residues and sedimentations from a life of experience with both the givens of the person's existential situation and the givens formed by unconscious remnants of early and later childhood experience shape a certain forceful expectation that provides a certain "hard" contour to the horizon possible for the person. But the language of image, metaphor, and myth or narrative provides a softer, more malleable and permeable conscious and preconscious formulation of the person's horizon of understanding of that situation. The two levels of language are connected in complex ways, and it is the task of the helping person to attend to both levels of language. It is important to keep in mind that, for Freud, access to the deeper layers of unconscious experience with its force dynamics was only possible through what he termed its "representations."

Herbert Fingarette, another philosopher whose work has given serious attention to the psychoanalytic tradition, proposes a slightly different formulation of the task of the therapeutic helper from that which develops from Ricoeur's reading of Freud. He suggests two possible definitions of the task, placing his emphasis on the second.[19] One definition characterizes the psychoanalytic therapeutic process as "the search for the hidden reality." Consciousness, in this formulation, is analogous to the quality of visibility. The therapeutic task lies in the opening of the "door hiding the hidden past," or the ripping of the veil from the "disguised present." A "hidden reality" must be found and unmasked, revealed. Change comes by the forced restructuring of the self made necessary by the revelation of these hidden realities.

In contrast to the "hidden reality" view, Fingarette proposes that the therapeutic helper, rather than searching with the client for the hidden reality of the past, offers a new interpretation of both past and present.

> The therapeutic insight does not show the patient what he is or was; it changes him into someone new. . . . Insight in its main function does not reveal unknown events of the past but helps us to see known past events in a new way. The phrase "unconscious process" does not refer directly to a spatio-temporal process. Insight into an unconscious wish is like noticing suddenly a well formed "ship" in the cloud instead of a poorly formed "rabbit." On the other hand, insight is not like discovering an animal which has been hiding in the bushes. Insight . . . is a reorganization of the meaning of present experience, a present reorientation toward both future and past.[20]

Here we come close to both Boisen's concept of the need for reorganization of the inner world of the suffering person and to Gadamer's fusion of horizons of understanding. Ricoeur's concept of the two levels of language, that of force and of meaning, enriches and extends the vision of both the language of inner subjective reality and of the task of bringing about change.

At this point I cannot resist inserting as a sort of experiential parenthetical comment the report of a recent dream I had. (My readers may take it as comic relief from an all too serious and abstract discussion, if they so desire!) The dream occurred at a seminary faculty retreat at which, during the evening session one of my theologian-philosopher colleagues, much more erudite in the philosophy of Paul Ricoeur than I, had presented a stimulating and, to me, intimidating discussion of some implications of Ricoeur's concept of the two languages for a theological consideration of the problem of human suffering. During the night in a strange bed I had apparently become too warm and kicked off the light covers, resulting in my getting chilled. I awoke cold and frightened after having a short but powerful dream. In the dream I awoke naked in a room with other persons present, and reached for the covers, which had slipped to the floor, so I could cover my nakedness. But as I started to pull the covers up around me, a fierce and powerfully ominous growl arose from the depths of the hidden floor at the other end of the blanket and a powerful pull was exerted to keep me from covering myself.

As I lay recovering my bearings upon awakening, the interpretation of the dream came to me that remains valid in my consciousness as I write of the experience. "To be warm and secure, I need to cover my nakedness and vulnerability with a blanket of meaning that gives coherence and mythic sense to my life. But always there is that deep and powerful, growling presence of the forces from the depths of my life that have shaped and continue to shape who I am. They lay bare my nakedness. The covering is so thin, and it keeps getting yanked away just when I need it. I am left exposed and vulnerable."

So it is with each of us. The language of the living human document we bring to any human encounter, be that an encounter with the texts that form the basis of our religious and cultural tradition or with other human beings, is a two-sided language. It is the language of the deep forces that have shaped our lives and given them contour and existential specificity. And it is also the language of our meaningful interpretation of our experience and its underlying forces. This latter language draws upon and makes use of the images and symbols, the myths and metaphors that have been made available to us by the sociocultural milieu from which we come. But it also has about it a certain twist and movement, a disposition, that marks it as uniquely and privately our own.

Given the elaboration on Boisen's living human document image that I have now undertaken, it is a major thesis of this book that Boisen was fundamentally correct in his placing of the crux of human spiritual suffering at the point of the connection between experience and idea, between the occurrence of events and a language of meaning for those events. It is when that connection becomes blocked, distorted, or made impossible that the troubled person must seek a helper, an interpreter who may offer a new possibility of meaning.

Construed in this fashion, the role of the pastoral counselor as interpreter and guide in the reconstruction of a structure and language of meaning on the part of the troubled person or persons takes on a profoundly religious, if not theological, cast. At the center of any structure of meaning lie the questions of faith and ultimate purpose. The age-old function of religion has been that of binding together all of life into some unitary vision that is finally meaningful. It is the authority and role of the principal representative of that function that the pastoral counselor brings to the task of interpretive guidance.

The problem that the contemporary pastoral counselor has as he or she approaches the task of interpretation and reinterpretation with troubled persons is, as has already been suggested, that pastoral counseling resides itself on the boundary of a number of language worlds. No one language world, even that of religion and theology, is in itself fully adequate for the task. Various language worlds must be integrated, while yet allowing each to function with its own integrity.

Language worlds may be imaged as themselves bridges between ambiguity and meaning. They link together the mysterious and unaccounted for, on the one side, and ordered intelligibility, on the other. Thus it may be said that, in the root meaning of the word, all language worlds have a religious or mythic function. They bind together what would otherwise remain fragmented and ambiguous. So the pastor, as religious counselor, may quite legitimately draw upon whatever language world may assist in the process of interpretation and reconstruction of the connections between experience and meaning for the troubled person. But the core and grounding language world on which pastoral counseling proceeds is the language of religion and faith. And it is to theological language that the pastor must turn to give rigor and structure to his or her use of religious as well as other language, though the spoken language of the therapeutic encounter may itself be that of metaphor and symbol, myth and story.

With this latter concern in mind, we now turn in the next chapter to a theological interpretation of the human situation formulated as the process of formation of a living human document that seeks to sustain its connection with those texts and documents that have shaped the Christian story and vision.

Pilgrimage, Incarnation, and the Hermeneutics of the Self

In the previous chapter I undertook a hermeneutical explication of Anton Boisen's symbolic formulation of the clinical pastoral task as the study of "living human documents." My initial purpose was to relate the task of interpretation of living human documents to the larger hermeneutical tradition by means of concepts and images that developed around the problems of interpretation of texts and other human artifacts. Not unexpectedly, it became clear that the problems of interpretation in pastoral counseling conversations have their parallels in the problems of interpretation considered by hermeneutical scholars. Some possible directions have emerged for potentially fruitful further exploration in the search for a valid base for pastoral counseling seen as an extension of the art and science of interpretation.

The beginning encounter with hermeneutical theory confronted me with the reality that interpretation always begins from a certain standpoint. It can only take place within the horizon of understanding of the interpreter. It is just at this point that the biblical and theological grounding for the pastoral counselor's self-understanding becomes crucial. It is that grounding which locates the unique perspective from which pastoral counselors are to make their interpretations. Without it pastoral counseling soon loses that primary orientation that makes the interpretive relationship pastoral.

Who one is as a pastoral counselor within the Christian tradition cannot be determined simply by introspective self-reflection. In Wilhelm Dilthey's language, our self-understanding as pastoral counselors requires a "hermeneutical detour," an excursion into reflection on those theological images and symbols that have given shape to Christian self-understanding historically. Not only is that the case for the pastoral counselor's own self-understanding, it likewise is necessary for a formation of an understanding of those whom we counsel. Our appropriation of the historical tradition within which we stand shapes a horizon of understanding from which we look as we view ourselves and other persons.

Any attempt at self-understanding by means of such a hermeneutical detour is, of necessity, inherently dialogical. The richness and variation of the Christian tradition offers a pluralism of symbolic images and historical themes from which to choose. Inevitably one's choices are influenced by one's own historical situation, written large in terms of one's time, and written small in terms of the particular contours of one's own life and practical purpose. The immediate questions that prompt the hermeneutical detour likewise exercise some selective power in determining which theological and biblical themes become formative. It is well, therefore, that before turning from the main road of our task in this book toward a hermeneutical detour, we sort over the images and issues we bring with us from our earlier brush with Boisen and hermeneutical theory. We also will need to clarify the situational factors that shape the approach of the pastoral counselor to biblical and theological materials.

One formative theme in the earlier work is, of course, the notion of particularity, both that of the living human document and the interpreter. That particularity theme has already presented us with the necessity of particularity in regard to the meaning of incarnation for which we seek verification from the biblical-theological tradition. To enter another's world requires getting inside the other's language world, with all the particularity and nuance that entails. But we also come with a deepened awareness of the particularity of the pastoral counselor and the limit that historical particularity places upon his or her ability to leave behind the unique perspective that forms the pastoral counselor's language world. A theme of desire and limit, possibility and horizon, thereby presents itself. That theme has expanded into one of self-understanding, both that of the pastoral counselor and that of the one seeking help, as involving a language of force and a language of meaning—a certain hard contour and a softer, more malleable human possibility of meaning. In turn, that theme focuses the human desire and question concerning change, its possibility and limit, the conditions necessary for its occurrence.

The question concerning God's participation in the process of human change was, in the hermeneutical work thus far, visible only in dim outline, since I was coming at the question from the human, rather than the Godward side. The desire to explore this question theologically in relation to the image of the activity of the Holy Spirit did, however, articulate itself.

The term "hermeneutical detour" I am using here, taken from Dilthey, may rest a bit uncomfortably in the reader's consciousness, as it does in mine. If taken to mean that any excursion into theology is, like a detour on the highway, an interference or an unnecessary departure from getting directly and expeditiously to the main task of pastoral counseling, then some other figure of speech would be preferable. A detour seen that way can soon become something one can very well do without as one moves ahead with the pragmatic task at hand. Dilthey meant the image of detour, however, to be taken as a quite necessary side trip in order properly to locate one's self-understanding. To use the term provided by Hans-Georg Gadamer, the *pre-understanding* that the pastoral counselor brings to the counseling situation needs to be self-consciously formed by serious dialogue with the tradition in which we desire our self-understanding to be rooted. Seen in that fashion, the "detour" becomes a necessity if the pastoral counselor's pre-understanding is to be authentically pastoral. Without the detour the dialogical road ahead in the counseling relationship will, figuratively speaking, be filled with blind spots and pitfalls. The detour is not an impediment, but a necessary facilitation of the movement toward deeper self-understanding and self-aware dialogue with the other person.

As a matter of fact, the image of the detour as a side trip, or a deviation from the direct route, rings true to the manner in which the pastoral counselor as pastoral counselor goes about his or her theological work. Theological reflection is not the main thing the pastoral counselor is about. What we are about is better described as ministry, which means, as Carroll Wise has stated it so clearly, that the pastoral counselor is concerned with the "communication of the inner meaning of the Gospel to persons at the point of their need."[1] Pastoral counseling is a relationship undertaken in the light of the gospel, not simply a statement of the gospel or a reflection on biblical or other statements of it. Thus, reflection on the objectifications of the Christian tradition as found in theology is, for pastoral counselors, a necessary movement "back" or "to the side" in order to get one's bearings and thus enable one better to fulfill one's central purpose.

Because I am a pastoral counselor I approach the biblical textual record and, for that matter, all other textual statements of the Judeo-Christian tradition in a fashion somewhat different from that of, for example, the biblical scholar or systematic theologian. As pastoral counselor I do not approach the biblical text with the purpose of developing a full, rich, and historically accurate exegesis, as one might do in the preparation of a sermon. Neither do I approach the historical or contemporary theological text with the purpose of formulating a full and carefully defended theological system, as would a systematic theologian. Rather I approach these texts of the tradition in search of images and themes, symbolic figurations and normative warrants that may prove formative for my ministry as pastoral counselor. I am alert for glimpses of analogy, stories, and images that, when interpreted in relation to my situation as pastoral counselor, may point a way or reveal a possibility as to what I am or should be about. I am also attentive to those themes and images that can reveal to me the richness of the tradition's understanding of the human condition and the range of human foibles and follies, as well as human desire and possibility. And I am constantly searching for clues to understanding the nature and purpose of God in his relationship to me and to my troubled counselees.

James D. and Evelyn E. Whitehead have usefully described this manner of approaching the Bible and other historic texts of the tradition in theological reflection as a search for "paradigms"— patterns and images that can "inform, influence, and inspire" ministers in relation to pastoral issues.[2] The Whiteheads include in their discussion of such paradigmatic images a rather lengthy quotation from James M. Gustafson that is so descriptive as to be well worth repeating here:

> Paradigms are basic models of a vision of life, and of the practice of life, from which flow certain consistent attitudes, outlooks (or "onlooks"), rules or norms of behavior, and specific actions. . . .
> Rather the paradigm *in*-forms and *in*-fluences the life of the community and its members as they become what they are under their own circumstances. By *in*-form I wish to suggest a formation of life. By *in*-fluence I wish to suggest a flowing into the life of the

community and its members. A paradigm allows for the community and its members to make it their own, to bring it into the texture and fabric of life that exists, conditioned as that is by its historical circumstances, by the sorts of limitations and extensions of particular capacities and powers that exist in persons and communities.[3]

Gustafson here helpfully suggests that biblical and theological paradigms must—if they are to shape a vision and practice of life, a self-understanding that is lived out in one's attitudes, outlook, and behavior—become endogenous in one's life. They form and flow in and through one's life so that the very texture and fabric of selfhood are made up of the interweaving of these paradigmatic images with the other, more historical, circumstantial and personal particularities that shape one's life. Thus paradigmatic images, though they have their origin outside the self in the antecedents of one's tradition, now are inside the self in ways that make them inseparable from who one is and the outlook or "onlook" of the self on the world.

Insofar as this inflowing and interweaving process has taken place, the use of paradigmatic images in one's self-reflection, one's reflection on relationships in the world, and one's activity as a person in the world does not have to be contrived or forced. They are simply present in the manner in which one's self and world understanding are experienced and expressed.

It is at this level that theological and biblical images, themes, and symbols need most significantly to function in the self-understanding and self-expression of the pastoral counselor. Doing the more formal intellectual work of theological reflection and interdisciplinary correlation is, of course, important and necessary. But pastoral counseling ministry seen as the communication of the inner meaning of the gospel to persons flows first out of that level of inner meaning that has been *in*formed and *in*fluenced by the paradigmatic images of faith.

As I reflect on my own life as a pastoral counselor, the image of a loose but definite set of interlocking connections comes to mind. At one nexus cluster the issues and continuing conversations with myself concerning the meaning and pilgrimage of my own life. At another nexus cluster the issues, questions, and dilemmas of my work as pastoral counselor, the flow of problems I encounter while in that situation of ministry. At yet another nexus cluster a host of images and themes or paradigms that have persistently become central to me in my continuous probing reflection on biblical and theological texts of the Christian tradition. These three clusters seem constantly involved in a kind of conversation with one another in my consciousness. Dreams and random associations at odd moments suggest to me that the conversation also goes on at deep levels of my being at an unconscious level. Thus, over time, what I am here calling a conversation among nexus clusters has *in*formed and *in*fluenced my self-understanding, both in the general sense and in terms of my self as pastoral counselor.

It may be helpful to schematize the inner conversational process that I am attempting to describe:

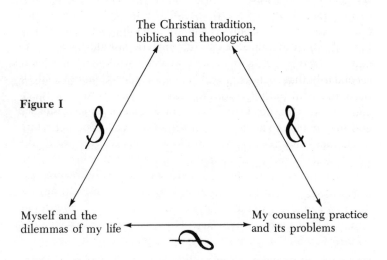

The Christian tradition,
biblical and theological

Figure I

Myself and the
dilemmas of my life

My counseling practice
and its problems

This schema suggests several things that are clarifying in understanding how the inner conversation of which I speak takes place. It suggests a certain tension and separation among the three arenas. Each has a certain separateness and integrity of its own. Thus, the Christian tradition nexus in a sense stands over against or is "other" from my self and the dilemmas of my life and from my counseling practice. Though certain of its images and themes have become endogenous to me and my counseling, it refuses to be collapsed into either of the other two nexuses. The same can be said of the other two clustering points. My self-understanding and my understanding of myself as pastoral counselor cannot be collapsed into or encompassed by each other; nor can either be collapsed into the tradition.

The feedback loops of the three sides of the schematic triangle suggest a continuous process of question and correction, refinement and integration. Thus the schema proposes both a dynamic and a flowing process. The image of a pilgrim seems to catch up the meaning to which the schema points, an image which, of course, is deeply rooted in the biblical tradition, but which also rings true to my life as a self and as a pastoral counselor.

Applying the image of pilgrimage to the schema of Figure I suggests that the pastoral counselor's "theological detour" may and does occur in an unsystematic or process fashion rather than being undertaken in an analytic style. This is not, of course, to say that the pastoral counselor does not at times approach theology or biblical interpretation in a careful, analytic fashion. Nor is it to diminish the importance of such analytic work. But it is only secondarily that such forms of theological reflection and analysis become useful to the pastoral counselor. What is more primary and formative for the life of the pastoral counselor is more informal and may even appear to the outside observer to be haphazard.

The sensitive pastoral counselor who tends carefully to the processes of his or her reflection on biblical and theological nexus materials in the search for self-understanding and direction will quickly become aware of a shift of language and mood from the more pragmatic, problem-solving language of the counseling situation. The here-and-nowness of the pastoral situation creates a context in which descriptive language and reasonable theoretical concepts come pragmatically into play. Theological reflection requires that we move to another, in certain ways quite different, level of language and imagination. In theological reflection a certain mystery and accompanying sense of awe and wonder at the ineffable presence of God in and through all events, processes in time, and relationships among persons and structures of reality define the context of one's awareness.

The great twentieth-century Jewish theologian Abraham Heschel points to this shift in context of awareness when he defines the awe of the religious person as "a way of being in rapport with the mystery of all reality."[4]

The meaning of awe is to realize that life takes place under wide horizons that range beyond the span of an individual life or even the life of a nation, a generation, or an era. Awe enables us to perceive in the world intimations of the divine, to sense in small things the beginning of infinite significance, to sense the ultimate in the common and the simple; to feel in the rush of the passing the stillness of the eternal.[5]

When one moves to this level of reflection on religious experience, one's own and that of the great figures of the religious tradition, one becomes aware that whatever language is used is somehow inadequate in that it fails fully to reveal that toward which it attempts to point one's awareness. That toward which it points is, to the human mind, finally ineffable. It can be spoken of only in the language of metaphor, myth, and symbol, not the hard, descriptive language of science or common sense. "By the ineffable we mean that aspect of reality which by its very nature lies beyond our comprehension, and is acknowledged by the mind to be beyond the scope of the mind."[6]

The first self-defining realization we come to, then, on our theological hermeneutical detour is that the horizon of understanding the pastoral counselor must attempt to bring to the counseling encounter is an awareness of the ineffable mystery of a horizon that is both ultimate (beyond our knowing) and awesomely present (incarnate) in and through all the events and processes in which we and our counselees participate.

It is from the biblical and theological tradition that we draw a broad range of images, symbols, and narrative themes that provide for us a language with which to reflect and, on occasion, to speak at this level of meaningful understanding. We are not here left entirely on our own, but rather we draw from the depths of our religious community and its tradition. The integrity of that tradition gives integrity to our perspective, granting it a shape and a controlling horizon. It is in the continued process of reflection on the multiform materials of the tradition in conjunction with reflection on the questions and issues encountered in the pastoral counseling situation that the pastoral counselor's practice of his or her art becomes informed and influenced by the ultimate perspective of the Christian faith.

The specificity of the pastoral counselor's appropriation of biblical-theological imagery in relation to counseling practice will,

as I have already indicated, be highly particular and relative to the
continuing issues and questions that preoccupy the individual's
attention. My own pilgrimage has, for reasons alluded to in
chapter 1, led me to focus my attention on questions concerning
the reality and nature of God's participation in the human
pilgrimage. Here I find myself identified at a deep level with the
biblical writers.

> To whom then will you liken God.
>   or what likeness compare with him?
>
> He does not faint or grow weary,
>   his understanding is unsearchable.
>   ISAIAH 40:18, 28 RSV
>
> For thou, O Lord, art my hope,
>   my trust, O Lord, from my youth.
> Upon thee I have leaned from my birth;
>   thou art he who took me from my
> mother's womb.
>   PSALM 71:5, 6 RSV

What do we and the people of the Bible have in common? The
anxieties and joys of living; the sense of wonder and the resistance
to it; the awareness of the hiding God and moments of longing to find
Him.

                                   ABRAHAM HESCHEL

In my earlier book, *Crisis Experience in Modern Life,* my own
critical theological questions growing out of pastoral work with
persons experiencing the crises of everyday life pressed me toward
images of a theology of incarnation—God's continuing activity on
human behalf—and of hope in the futurity of the kingdom of God
as a basis for my pastoral identity.[7] Following Wolfhart
Pannenberg, God's providential care was seen as that "power of
the future which we are persuaded is trustworthy."[8] Human life,
lived always in the tension of the present, caught between past and
future, is best lived as life open to the power of the future. Such a
life requires a continuous process of transformation as old human
structures of meaning and relationship are carried over and
trans-formed by the inbreaking power of the open-ended future.
Again, the image of life as pilgrimage comes to the fore as an
organizing image of human life under God. Meaning in the

ultimate sense is meaning transformed by the power of God that breaks open all human structures of meaning, rendering them provisional and temporary.

The image of the providential power of God as a power that draws us out of the past and orients our life toward the future has been for me a potent image in my struggle in pastoral counseling with my own and my counselee's tendencies to become mired down in the patterns of life of the past. It is an image that makes possible a degree of hope for change even when all visible concrete evidence points to its impossibility.

It is not my purpose in this chapter to deal with all the questions and issues that the pastoral counselor takes with him or her into the dialogue with the biblical and theological tradition or the wide range of issues one finds when one enters that dialogue. Rather, I would propose at this point to return to the problem of change as we encountered it in the previous chapter. What do we find helpful to us in making a theological detour with that question in mind? What of the ambiguous tension between what, following Ricoeur, I called the language of force and the language of meaning with regard to change? Does the God of the future that I bring from my previous theological and pastoral work run head on into the hard contours of force that shape human selfhood? From a theological standpoint within the Christian tradition, what can be said about the ambiguities, the stubborn problem of change?

Paul Tillich, my first theological mentor, comes at this question out of his formulation of Christian existence. The hard, unchanging contour of human life is, for Tillich, the existential reality of finitude. There is a fundamental ambiguity about all things human simply because we are finite creatures. Self-integration, the possibility of unity within the self, and thus change that moves toward unity, is limited by our finite nature. The purpose of created life is the actualization of that life's potentials. Yet no human life can actualize all its potentialities. Self-identity is relational. It involves a taking into the self of "contents of the encountered world." To refuse to allow the new content from outside to enter the centered self is to become an empty self. Yet to open one's self too easily to change is to risk a chaotic self-identity. "And the basic question is: How many potentialities given to me by virtue of my being man, and, further, by being this particular man, *can* I actualize without losing the power to actualize anything seriously? And, how many of my potentialities *must* I actualize in order to avoid the state of mutilated humanity?"[9]

Tillich's theological "solution" to the problem rests in his understanding of the "Spiritual Presence," although he acknowledges that it is a partial, fragmentary solution still subject to the limits of finite life. "Where Spiritual Presence is effective, life is turned into the direction which is more than one direction among others—the direction toward the ultimate within all directions. This direction does not replace the others but appears within them as their ultimate end and therefore as the criterion of the choice between them."[10] It is through the power of the Spiritual Presence that human self-identity is changed, bringing about a new multidimensional unity to a life that was previously disunified and fragmented.[11] Though life remains not fully transformed, as the universe remains not yet transformed, "the Spirit transforms actually in the dimension of the Spirit. Men are the 'first fruits' of the New Being; the universe will follow them."[12]

Let us here make a tentative move toward a rough, but useful, integration of the languages of Tillich and of Ricoeur's interpretation of Freud. Though their purposes are very different, there is a rough correspondence between the hard language of force, as Ricoeur uses that concept, and the language of finitude and its limits, as Tillich develops that language. It is the forceful limit of human historical finitude that provides what in chapter 2 we termed the hard, not easily changed contours of our lives. Further, Tillich's theological understanding of the power of the Spiritual Presence proposes a level at which change under that power becomes possible. Can we make a further rough correlation between Ricoeur's language of meaning and Tillich's language of actual change at the level of human spirit?

> The multidimensional unity of life means that the impact of the Spiritual Presence in the human spirit is *at the same time* an impact on the *psyche*, the cells, and the physical elements which constitute man. And although the term "impact" unavoidably uses causal imagery, it is not a cause in the categorical sense but a presence which participates in the object of its impact. Like the divine creativity in all respects, it transcends the category of causality, although human language must make use of causality in a symbolic way.[13]

Here Tillich acknowledges the mystery of the Spiritual Presence and our inability to speak of it in language other than the inadequate language of impact, cause, or force. It has its impact on the physical elements, or, we might say, the hard contours of our lives, but its impact is one that "participates in" those hard contours to bring a new unity and direction to them. It is as if the forces of our lives remain the same, yet have a new flow and direction because of the unifying power of the Spiritual Presence. Tillich in this fashion presses us toward a new synthesis of the force-meaning language dichotomy we have brought with us from the hermeneutical work of chapter 2.

Jurgen Moltmann, the contemporary German theologian whose theology combines serious attention to the textual authority of the biblical language concerning God's activity in creation and history with concern for human liberation, offers us a somewhat different set of paradigmatic images with which to consider the problem of human change. His purpose, however, is quite similar to that of Tillich. He, too, recognizes the mystery and ambiguity involved in any human understanding of the activity of God in human processes of change.

For Moltmann the history of human life and the trinitarian history of God are closely intertwined. The possibilities and limits of the human situation are defined by the limits of our human location within the history of God's life within himself in the times between creation and the fulfillment of God's kingdom. "The deliverance of the world from its contradiction is nothing less than God's deliverance of himself from the contradiction of his world."[14] Thus the human pilgrimage takes place within the pilgrimage of God in his trinitarian history. Moltmann understands the biblical record as "the testimony to the history of the Trinity's relations of fellowship, which are open to men and women, and open to the world. This trinitarian hermeneutics leads us to think in terms of relationships and communities; it supersedes the subjective thinking which cannot work without the separation and isolation of its objects."[15] Moltmann thus attempts to develop a style of thinking "ecologically about God, man and the world in their relationships and indwellings."[16] The image of the self as subject within an objective set of forces is replaced by an image of a history of relationships within God and within creation, including human relationships.

The paradigmatic biblical image of pilgrimage becomes in Moltmann's treatment a corporate, relational image involving God in his relationships within himself and likewise involving creation and the human involvement in creation. All are in pilgrimage and interacting movement. Within that primary image of the pilgrimage of the whole of things, including God, a further organizing image is that of suffering. The history of God is the history of his love and suffering. Suffering thus replaces power and omnipotence as the primary characteristic of God. That suffering image comes into focus most clearly in the event of the cross in which God's suffering takes two forms: that of Jesus, the Son, who suffers abandonment, and that of God the Father, who suffers in the act of abandonment. [17] But the image of suffering fulfills a larger role than simply that of the meaning of the Cross; it becomes the image for the ongoing presence and relationship of God to his creation and to all things human. Jesus, the Logos, is to be sought wherever there is human suffering. His identification is with all who suffer and long for redemption from their bondage to the forces of history. Likewise, the Spirit is to be found wherever there is suffering in the not-yet-ness of the final unity of all things both within God and within his creation. "The spirit of God makes the impossible possible; he creates love where there is nothing lovable; he creates hope where there is nothing to hope for. . . . The Spirit of God works in history as the creator of a new future and as the new creator of what is transient for this future."[18]

In Moltmann's trinitarian theology, human existence, because it is caught up in the trinitarian history of God's relationship to his creation, is paradoxical. It involves "at the same time" both the empirical existence of history and the eschatological reality of the coming Kingdom made present in the saving event of the cross.[19] Human identity is therefore paradoxical. It involves our human embeddedness in the historical process both as individuals and as members of an interacting set of corporate relationships in creation. Individual identity is, for Moltmann, relational identity, not simply the identity of a discrete and separate subjective self. Both our historical and eschatological identity are therefore caught up in and participate in an ecologically corporate process.

The paradigmatic image of the paradoxical identity of the self, when appropriated as the controlling theological image for consideration of the problem of change in pastoral counseling, can be shown to have a salutary effect in a number of ways. Like Ricoeur's language of force and Tillich's language of the limits of finitude, it provides a check on our human wishes for change that so erases all our ties to the past and to the circumstances of our lives that continuity is lost and the self becomes unrecognizable. Every human life is embedded in a personal and corporate history that gives that life a unique configuration and continuity. At times that historical embeddedness is experienced as an intractable problem from which the person would like to leap or be rescued. But the same embeddedness gives definiteness and particularity to each individual life and its linkages to the whole ecology of creation.

The other side of paradoxical identity is, for Moltmann, the potential for the individual to participate, albeit fragmentarily and provisionally, in life under the reality of the coming of the kingdom of God. "We can already live in the light of the 'new era' in the circumstances of the 'old' one."[20] Life under the power of the eschatological identity is life transformed in its meaning and direction because it is life experienced as participant in the power of the coming Kingdom in which all things are made new. Thus the memory of historical life is linked in dialectical tension with the anticipation of the life that is to come. Moltmann's term for such a life is "messianic." "Just as the messianic era stands under the token of 'not yet,' so it also stands under the sign of 'no longer' and therefore under the sign of 'already.' "[21]

Life lived under the power of both sides of the paradoxical identity is both life lived with suffering and with hopeful anticipation. "We know that the whole creation has been groaning in travail together until now, and not only the creation, but we ourselves, who have the first fruits of the Spirit, groan inwardly as we wait for adoption as sons, the redemption of our bodies. For in this hope we are saved" (Romans 8:22, 23, 24 RSV).

Persons coming for pastoral counseling are usually aware of the suffering that comes from their embeddedness in their history. Their understanding of the history of their suffering is most often cloudy and may itself contribute to their suffering. They often come seeking freedom from their embeddedness in a new life free from suffering. Not infrequently their awareness of the sources of their suffering is sharpened and clarified in the course of counseling conversations. But also not infrequently they are disappointed to find that the counseling relationship does not remove their suffering to their satisfaction. Rather it only makes possible new ways of coming to grips with the issues of their lives that are bound up in their suffering. The suffering of frustration at the seemingly intractable circumstances of their lives is gradually replaced by the suffering of frustration at the possibilities and limits of change.

The theological paradigmatic image of human paradoxical identity suggests that one way to consider the predicament of the suffering person who comes for counsel is to see him or her as having become separated from the meaning of our human eschatological identity. The hermeneutic of hope and expectation can become lost or overshadowed by images of selfhood and relationships that emerge from one's history. In a later chapter we will explore a concept of the emergence of myths of the self and the world in the course of individual development. These mythic images and themes frequently do not include, or only nebulously include, an understanding of the self as having what, following Moltmann, we are here calling an eschatological identity. Here one purpose of pastoral counseling comes into view, that of restoring persons to an awareness of our eschatological identity within the history of God in relation to God's creation and in anticipation of the coming Kingdom. Change, seen in this framework, involves such an alteration in the mythic images of the self that the dialectical tension between the self in its history and the self as participant in the eschatological future is restored or made more clearly operative in the person's self-understanding. Once again in Moltmann's thought, as in Tillich's, we are pressed toward a new theological coalescence between the language of force and the language of meaning.

From the theological standpoint, the problem of human change has been seen historically as an aspect of the problem of human freedom. In pastoral counseling the problem of freedom becomes concretely visible as the counselee, having gained fresh insight into his or her historical and existential situation, now confronts the anxious necessity of putting insight into action in behavior and altered relationships. Often freedom seems limited and the compulsion to repeat old patterns powerful. What, theologically speaking, in that situation does it mean to be free? Within Moltmann's trinitarian hermeneutic, this question is linked to the question of faith in the power of the coming kingdom of God. To be free in the situation described is to act upon hope. Moltmann calls this kind of freedom a passion for the future in the power of the Spirit. "In the Spirit we transcend the present in the direction of God's future, for the Spirit is the 'earnest' or 'pledge of glory.'"[22] Said another way, the freedom to change is dependent, theologically speaking, on the appropriation of the self's eschatological identity in the power of the Spirit.

It must be remembered that the paradoxical, "at the same time" quality of paradoxical identity remains true for the person who risks acting on the hope of the eschatological identity as was the case before the risking of the freedom. The exercise of freedom then becomes a kind of project or relationship to a project, rather than a state of being in which one is free to act without constraint.[23] Freedom, therefore, involves the commitment of one's future into the trinitarian history of God.

Like Tillich, Moltmann sees change in the self as involving the work of the Spirit. The Spirit is seen as "an energy or power whose subject is God or Christ."[24] The presence of the Spirit is to be found in all processes and experiences in which and through which eschatology and history are mediated.[25] The pastoral counselor, working as one informed by that paradigmatic image seeking to bring about change, will place final confidence in the power and work of the Spirit rather than in whatever human influence he or she may be able to exercise. All that is humanly possible should be done to facilitate the creation of a relationship in which the possibility is opened. By the power of the Spirit, mediating change may take place. But change should not, indeed cannot, be forced or finally accomplished by the counselor's human effort. From that burden we as pastoral counselors are relieved.

Pastoral counseling has long recognized and made paradigmatic use of the biblical theological symbol of incarnation as a formative image giving purpose and definition to the relationship of the pastoral counselor to the person seeking help.[26] The analogy of God's incarnation in Jesus here becomes the controlling paradigmatic image for the grace and acceptance the counseling relationship is to embody. It thus provides a structuring image for the intentionality of the pastoral counselor. As a member and representative of the body of Christ the pastoral counselor seeks to embody the quality of relationship that fulfills the incarnational analogy.

The theological hermeneutical detour we have just taken into the tradition's mythic understanding of the work of the Spirit as formulated by Paul Tillich and Jurgen Moltmann suggests an important extension and correction of the incarnational imagery. Here we are no longer simply working with a controlling analogy. Rather, the counseling relationship is itself seen as subject to the power of the Spirit at work in the mediation between history and eschatology. The counselor does not, indeed cannot, by an act of intentionality embody the Spirit. The counseling relationship is rather subject to the Spiritual Presence upon whom any movement toward reappropriation of the eschatological identity, any fragmentary experience of the new reality of the Kingdom, finally depends.

Seen as a relationship subject to the power of the Spirit, the pastoral counseling relationship is set free to be what it is: a human relationship between or among persons seeking new understanding and direction for life. It is a relationship undertaken in hope and with the expectation that in the search for new directions the seekers will be accompanied by the Spirit exercising God's mediating power.

As I write these paragraphs, I recognize what may appear to be a potentially confusing mixture of descriptive, "empirical" language and highly symbolic language that points to the ineffable mystery of the working of God in human affairs. To attempt a theological description of the pastoral counseling relationship or the process of change that such a relationship seeks, inevitably risks the confusion of the levels of language. In a later chapter, I will develop a typology of language levels pertinent to pastoral counseling as a way of ordering that potential confusion. At this point it must suffice simply again to acknowledge that such theological "descriptions" can only be undertaken within a mythic language that points to what is finally ineffable and mysterious, albeit powerfully disclosive.

Viewed theologically, the pastoral counseling methodological problem that emerges from these reflections may be seen as involving the arts of both facilitation and recognition. Facilitation has to do with the counselor's human effort to facilitate the appropriation of a paradoxical identity in the pilgrimage of the person seeking counsel. It involves the question as to what, from the human, ministering side, may best be said or done or embodied in the person of the counselor to open the way for the mediating work of the Spirit. Stated in the language of hermeneutics, the problem may be seen as that of so relating to the other person that the hermeneutic of the self embedded in history may be transformed into a hermeneutic that appropriates the good news of God's participation in the life of the person on his or her behalf through the power of the Spirit.

Pastoral counseling as facilitation includes the relationship of the counselor to both sides of the human identity paradox. Certainly the historical identity, both in its particular, personal dimensions and in its social, situational dimensions, must be given its proper attention. As a matter of fact, it is to this task that much of the so-called therapeutic emphasis of pastoral counseling in recent years has been directed. But the facilitating work of pastoral counseling with regard to opening the way for a meaningful appropriation or reappropriation of the human eschatological identity—the identity of the self within the trinitarian history of God's activity in creation—is of equal importance. Just how that facilitative task is to be undertaken demands further consideration in later chapters. Here I simply point to the paradoxical, two-sided nature of the pastoral counseling task that corresponds to the two-sided paradox of human identity within the Christian vision.

As an expression of the art of recognition, pastoral counseling has as one of its central focuses the sensitizing of both counselor and counselee to those occasions of relationship and experience, events and symbolic connections in which intimations of the presence and activity of the Spirit are to be recognized. Following Tillich, the Spiritual Presence is not seen as a "cause" or "force" alongside other dynamic forces in the living experience of the participants in the counseling relationship. Rather the Spirit may be recognized as participant in those forces and interactions, giving them a new direction that opens up a more nearly free and hopeful future.[27]

Jurgen Moltmann's concept of the human paradoxical identity is useful as an organizing image for pastoral counseling at still another point now subject to some controversy in the field. As stated earlier, both sides of paradoxical identity are, in Moltmann's thinking, to be understood in corporate, ecological terms. The history of the self is linked inextricably to the history of all creation. Historical identity formation is therefore not simply an individual, private, subjective process. Not only is this true with regard to the historical and relational forces that shape historical identity; it is also true in regard to the interpretive meanings that are attached to these forces in the history of the self. Meaning arises out of the interactions and interrelationships of the self embedded in a world of meaning. Likewise, the side of the self Moltmann calls the eschatological identity is a corporate, ecological, relational identity. Laying claim to and participating in the eschatological identity of the coming Kingdom is dependent upon a corporate, ecological process involving not only one's fellow human beings, but also the ecology of relationships within God.

Yet there is in Moltmann's concept something of the particularity and uniqueness of the individual. Both historical and eschatological identity have a a particular only-once-in-all-time-and-history quality about them. Thus, what appears to be another paradox comes into view—the paradox of particularity in an ecology of relationships. At the same time that human self-identity is wrapped up in a whole range of connections, historical and eschatological, that identity is also a unique self project given shape and meaning by the self's own interpretive and responsive process.

One of the current controversies in the field of pastoral care and counseling has to do with whether the pastor in his or her caring function should be primarily concerned with the facilitation of a climate or ethos of care within the corporate community of faith and life or be primarily engaged in relating on a one-to-one basis with persons who have particular problems of living. Is the ecology or the particularity of human care and suffering to be the primary focus of ministry? This controversy is, of course, only one aspect of a much larger tension that is manifested all through Western society at both theoretical and practical levels. It is at the root of the controversy between psychoanalytic and systems psychologies. It lies beneath the tension between social and political ethics, on the one hand, and an ethic of character and responsibility, on the other. The tension between an existentialist and a political-liberationist theological stance likewise contains this controversy of perspectives.

By building a theological stance on the images of the double paradox of historical-eschatological identity and particularity-ecology or individual-private and corporate-cultural, I will be attempting in these pages to build a tentative and perhaps fragile bridge between both sides of the deep, multifaceted controversy described in the previous paragraph. Just as both historical and eschatological identity must be engaged in the counseling relationship, so also must the particularity of individual subjectivity and the ecological, corporate relationship of the forces that both shape life and give it meaning.

The question of human change in the context of pastoral counseling itself contains this double paradox when considered through the lens of the paradigmatic theological images I have developed, building upon the existentialist theology of Paul Tillich and the trinitarian-ecological thought of Jurgen Moltmann. An understanding of change must thus embrace both sides of the double paradox. Change involves changing the self in relation to its place and process in its history. Change also involves the appropriation of the self's connection to the trinitarian history of God. Change alters the self in its existential self-understanding. Lasting change also is only possible in a context of changed relationships and shared meanings. It is the task of the pastoral counseling relationship to concern itself with the issues and possibilities that emerge in all four aspects of the double paradox.

As we come to the end of our theological hermeneutical detour, one further clarifying reflection comes into view flowing from the image of the double paradox of human identity theologically considered. The process we have been through in this chapter clearly and firmly grounds pastoral counseling in the life and mission of the church as the arena in which the four sides of the double paradox may be most carefully and responsibly tended. Pastoral counseling, as I have here given it a theological self-understanding, cannot fulfill its identity as a private relationship between a helper and a troubled person in an otherwise secular context apart from the church. Rather, pastoral counseling is by its very nature, as understood through the hermeneutical tools here developed, a function and mission within the church. In the best sense, pastoral counseling may thus be seen to have an eschatological and evangelical purpose. It is an aspect of the church's mission to celebrate the good news of the incarnation and be responsive to the reconciling work of the Spirit in the world. No matter what the physical location of the pastoral counselor's encounter with the suffering of persons may be, it is within the relational meaning context of the church that the four-sided paradox may be properly given attention. It is that context which provides the ecology of meaning in which the pastoral counselor participates and to which he or she invites the suffering person. And it is on the Christian vision of both history and the eschatological work of the Spirit that *pastoral* counseling finally depends, no matter what descriptive language the pastoral counselor may use in the process of interpretation of what is seen and experienced in the counseling room.

Having completed our theological hermeneutical detour, we shall turn in the next chapter to the task of exploration of some of the languages of psychotherapeutic psychology in search of possible connecting links between the theological language world from which we come and the images and themes of that very different, if contiguous, world. The connecting links we may locate will not be direct and literal. In a sense we enter a world with a very different set of mythic images at its core. Yet there may appear links upon which a meaningful dialogue may take place and our understanding of the pastoral counseling task be enriched.

Ego Psychology, Object Relations Theory, and the Hermeneutics of the Self

At the center of the branch of therapeutic psychology springing from Sigmund Freud's work are two primary images that pastoral counselors have come virtually to take for granted: the images of developmentalism and conflict within the self. The extent to which these two formative images for psychological interpretation have affected pastoral counseling modes of interpretation has been so great that, in the minds of many pastors, counseling persons and helping persons to deal with conflicts or to grow have virtually become synonymous. The self in conflict and the self seeking to grow and outgrow old conflicts have become the images of the person who is the object of pastoral counseling.

Freud formulated his vision of the human individual as pessimistic and tragicomic.[1] His theory of the instinctual drives seeking gratification but thrown into conflict with the "civilizing" power and authority of the parents turned his vision toward both a developmental hermeneutic and a concept of the self as subject to conflicting forces within and in relation to the self. As Freud envisioned them on the basis of his clinical work, the drives themselves are continuously in conflict. This is true whether we are referring to early Freud's formulation of the libidinous or sexual drive and the self-preservative drive or to later Freud's proposal of the perpetual struggle between Eros and Thanatos. Furthermore, not only is the individual subject to parental authority in the parental response to behavior prompted by the drives in actual events of childhood development, but, even more important, the parents become the most significant figures in the child's imaginative fantasy. Here we catch a glimpse of the rich significance of our earlier discussion, in chapter 2, of Ricoeur's interpretation of Freud as involving both a language of force and of meaning. Although Freud retained throughout his work a primary concern for both internal and external "forces" that shape the personality of the child, by recognizing the power of the young child's fantasied relation to the parental figures by way of their imagined representations, Freud placed strong emphasis on the child's own privately meaningful interpretations of these relationships and pointed to their symbolic significance. The kernel of a concept of the individual self as imaginative interpreter of his or her own experience here comes into view, though Freud himself never used that language.

Freud's personality theory is often given a more mechanical, deterministic reading than this brief sally into its inner workings would indicate. Freud's own language is often mechanical, as, for example, his use of the term "mechanism" to denote the ego's efforts to defend itself against the various forces bombarding it. His scientific mind-set, given the time in which he wrote, dictated a certain mechanistic, cause-effect flavor for his explanations of human phenomena. Yet, from very early in his theoretical efforts, he was attracted to the more mysterious and less materialistic power of the symbolic—that which at multiple layers could be understood as containing interpretable clusters of often conflicting meaning in representations. In fact, Freud proposed that it was only in the form of symbolic representations that the instinctual drives were themselves made available to the external observer. The more deeply Freud moved into his project seeking to understand what he observed in his patients as *psychic* phenomena, the more deeply he became committed to a symbolic understanding of mental life.

It will be useful for our purpose of understanding the force/meaning language mix in psychoanalytic thought to review some of the history of the development of the concept of ego. Although Freud in his structural theory of the various agencies or "institutions" of the self postulated the ego as a central arbitrator of the various dynamic forces shaping the life of the developing individual, it remained for certain of his second- and third-generation followers to develop this core idea. Freud's developmentalism had by this time become fully established so that theory about the ego and its functioning followed the familiar pattern of theory about the ego's formation in the life of the developing child. But for Freud's ego psychologist followers, the ego became much more than simply the perceiving and compromising arbitrator among its several "masters": the drives, the internalized parental authority of the superego, and the pleasure and reality principles.

Sigmund Freud's daughter, Anna, became a key figure in the early investigations of Freud's followers into the functions of the ego from a psychoanalytic perspective. Anna Freud did not, in terms of its core images, revise her father's basic conceptualizations, but she did greatly elaborate on them. In her major work, *The Ego and Mechanisms of Defense*, she says of the symbolizing function of the ego:

> We remember that in psycho-analytical metapsychology the association of affects and instinctual processes with ideas of words is stated to be the first and most important step in the direction of the mastery of instinct which has to be taken as the individual develops. Thinking is described in these writings as "an experimental process in which the smallest possible quantities of instinct are employed." This intellectualization of instinctual life, the attempt to lay hold on the instinctual processes by connecting them with ideas which can be dealt with in consciousness, is one of the most general, earliest and most necessary acquirements of the human ego. We regard it not as an activity of the ego but as one of its indispensable components.[2]

Here we see a clear point of connection with the Boisen paradigm from which we began the work of this book. Like Boisen, Anna Freud places emphasis on the ability to connect idea with depth dynamic experience, "one of the most general, earliest and most necessary requirements of the human ego." From early in life the ego must make interpretations. For Anna Freud, these interpretations must "lay hold on the instinctual processes" in ways that make them manageable, even useful, in the life of the self.

Heinz Hartmann, one of the leaders of the New York school of psychoanalysts in the 1930s and 40s, builds upon Anna Freud's work but takes a somewhat different tack. Hartmann, in a landmark essay first presented in 1937, *Ego Psychology and the Problem of Adaptation*, proposes, alongside these aspects of ego functioning dominated by conflicts derivative of the drives, what he terms a "conflict-free sphere" of ego functioning. Within this sphere all those aspects of human development related to growth and the expanding exposure of the child to the environment function in the formation of a relatively strong or weak ego more or less able to cope with both the drive-related conflicts and the growth tasks of the conflict-free sphere.

> Ego strength—though it manifests itself strikingly in the struggles of the conflict-sphere—cannot be defined solely in terms of that borderland of the ego which is involved in the conflict. . . . Once we have determined objectively those factors of ability, character, will, etc., which are the empirical—not theoretical—correlates of "strong" or "weak" egos, we will have escaped the relativity of the usual definitions which determine ego strength from the individual ego's relation to its id or superego.[3]

I have rehearsed this history of classical psychoanalytic ego psychology for several reasons. First, it is important to place Anton Boisen's developing image of the living human document and his idea concerning the crucial psychological importance of the connection between idea and experience in the context of contemporaneous developments in self or ego psychology. Boisen was quite obviously not alone in his concern for the connection between meaning and experience. Second, I want to establish in the psychoanalytic literature of that period a possible connection, albeit undeveloped and unacknowledged, with the less self-consciously psychological hermeneutical literature with which we were working in chapter 2. What I am reaching for here is the teasing out of a possible connection within psychoanalytic ego psychology to Boisen's hermeneutical notion of the self as interpreter of its own experience. To be sure, connections need to be made between this idea and dynamic conflict theory, if we are to remain in dialogue with psychoanalysis; but, if we are to escape the hard determinism of a mechanistic reading of psychoanalytic thought, a basis must be found within ego psychology for the spontaneous interpretive role of the ego. Behind the desire to find that basis lies the pastoral theological desire to relate to the person seeking our help as to one who is seeking anew to interpret, make new sense out of, his or her experience of life while at the same time taking full account of the dynamic forces involved, which modern pastoral care has so effectively emphasized. If we are to understand our ministry as related to a personal living human document, the process of authorship itself needs to be established.

From a psychological perspective, following Freud's developmental paradigm, my concern for establishing authorship of the living human document leads us deeper into questions concerning the origins of the sense of self. Here we encounter several post-Freudian theorists who have emerged as analysts working within the psychoanalytic tradition. They have been pressed to extend their developmental investigations into earlier periods of infantile life than that of the Oedipal period which so greatly preoccupied Freud. Generally speaking, these mostly third-generation neo-Freudians can be lumped together under the general title of object relations theorists.

Freud's conflict and drive theories were developed in large part out of his clinical encounter with the troubled people of Victorian Europe. That time was a time of both sexual inhibition and the beginning of breakdown of patriarchal authority, a breakdown which has by our time come full blown upon Western society. Freud's anxious, hysterical, conflict-ridden clientele led him to produce a theory that, while it recognized the importance of earlier childhood development, focused heavily on the psycho-*sexual* formation of the Oedipal period. Occurring ordinarily sometime between the ages of five and seven, the Oedipal period was seen by Freud as a time of strong sexual and identity conflict when the forces of the drives came into sharp confrontation with the power and authority of the parents. Most of Freud's work with the notions of symbolism and fantasy centered around this stage of development, as did his work with the force conflicts of the drives.

The object relations theorists have turned their attention toward the earliest experiences of the infant, beginning with birth. There are numerous reasons that could be proposed for this concentration on the earliest human experiences. The most significant, from a broad cultural perspective, are probably two: (1) the need to understand the origins of the psychoses, most particularly the schizophrenias, and (2) the increasing number of persons seeking psychotherapeutic help whose problems, rather than being those of neurotic conflict, seem to have more to do with the emptiness and lack of self-regard that accompany an absence of a sturdy sense of self. These latter problems are often characterized as problems of narcissism, either in the grandiose sense or in the sense of grandiosity's opposite, self-denigration.

The term "object relations" is an extension of Freudian language in which the term "object" is used primarily to designate a person in the environment toward which the individual develops a significant attitude or relationship. The concept also applies, however, to other sorts of objects, such as places or institutions. The primary object relationship is obviously with the mother, followed somewhat later by the father and/or siblings.[4]

The object relations paradigm begins with the notion, formulated both out of actual observation of infants and mothers and out of analytic work with adults, that in the preverbal stage of infancy the self and object world are fused. In that earliest situation it is therefore appropriate to speak of "self-objects," nascent image fragments in which the dichotomy of self and other does not yet exist. So helpless and unable to initiate response is the infant that the mother in particular tends to provide that active response to the child that anticipates every discomfort or need the child may experience. Child and mother, child and world, are one and the same. The process most often called separation-individuation by object relations theory has not yet begun.

But this paradise cannot last. Physically separated from the mother by birth, the infant begins very early to have experiences that contradict this unity of self and object world. The mother's face appears and disappears. Despite her attentions, the discomforts of hunger and wetness make their appearance. A new situation has intruded itself. Object relations writers speak of this time as one of enormous potential anxiety. As yet lacking any language or reality sense with which to encompass or "understand" this new experience, the infant may only have a vague and unnamed awareness of threat as if falling or exploding into nothingness.

As one might anticipate, the key question here posed to the object relations theorist is, How does the preverbal sense of the self as separate from mother and the world take form? How does the infant first leave the symbiosis of self and object world and begin the process of becoming a separate, self-conscious individual?

Object relations theories have various ways of speaking about this problem. Recognizing that there are a number of significant differences among them, I have found the ideas of three theorists, each doing his work in somewhat different contexts and out of slightly different theoretical backgrounds, most useful in putting together the psychological undergirding for a hermeneutical theory of pastoral counseling. We will look then briefly at the thought of D. W. Winnicott, Otto Kernberg, and Heinz Kohut.

D. W. Winnicott (1896–1971) was a prolific contributor to the "British school" of object relations theorists. Trained as a Freudian psychoanalyst, Winnicott was a London pediatrician who specialized in working with children and their mothers. Thus his writings tend to emerge directly from his active clinical practice, and they have about them a certain reflective, rambling, and very human quality.

Winnicott took Freud's drive conflict theory for granted. But he also believed that conflict theory must be linked to a prior concern for the developing self. The instincts for him became forces exerting their energy on a central self. "The central self could be said to be the inherited potential which is experiencing a continuity of being, and acquiring in its own way and at its own speed a personal psychic reality and a personal body scheme."[5]

For Winnicott the central self goes through a three-stage process in beginning its formation as separate from the mother: absolute dependence, relative dependence, and a stage Winnicott called "toward independence." In the stage of absolute dependence the infant knows nothing of maternal care or its absence; the infant only suffers or experiences pleasure. But with the passage of time the infant begins to become fragmentarily aware of the details of mother's care and begins to a limited extent to relate awareness of these details to what is experienced and to the impulses that are associated with experiences of pleasure or pain. Still later the infant self becomes sufficiently separate and self-aware to do without actual care for a time. Memories of care received in the recent past begin to take form, and trust in the return of care in the future begins to develop.

Winnicott speaks of a "line of life" beginning in this early period which has continuity and begins to integrate all that the infant experiences, though the infant vascillates between a state of relative integration and unintegration. Life begins to have for the child a flavor of "going on being" which leads to the nascent sense of "I am."

First comes "I" which includes "everything else is not me." Then comes "I am, I exist. I gather experiences and enrich myself and have an introjective and projective interaction with the NOT-ME, the actual world of shared reality." Add to this: "I am seen or understood to exist by someone;" and, further, add to this: "I get back (as a face seen in a mirror) the evidence I need that I have been recognized as a being."[6]

Understandably, Winnicott emphasizes the significance of the quality of mothering the child receives during this beginning of the sense of self as separate from the world, especially the crucial importance of the "good-enough mother." This is not the theoretically perfect mother who is so able to anticipate the infant's every need that the terrifying anxiety of separation is never felt. Rather, the good-enough mother is the one whose response to the child is adequate to provide some assurance of her presence while yet gradually communicating her separateness.

In terms of our developing hermeneutical theory, there are at least two deep-lying psychological anchors for the theory to be found in Winnicott's formulation of the beginnings of the sense of self. Winnicott has first given us a psychological base line for our hermeneutical understanding of the self as interpreter of its own experience. From the time of earliest beginnings of separation into a self-aware being, the human individual is in the situation of having to establish continuity of existence and differentiation of self from world through what in a real, if rudimentary sense may be called "interpretations." Why does the mother's face disappear? Why does it return? What is this that seems other than myself? Preverbally, nascently, fragmentarily, the self must make sense of that situation and cope with the anxiety of its mystery. Winnicott points here to the importance of a brief, passing stage of experienced omnipotence, as if the ebb and flow of care received were under the infant's control, if the anxiety of that beginning situation is to be managed and a sense of continuity of self established.[7]

The second deep-set psychological anchor Winnicott's theory provides is that this interpretive process of the self is, from the beginning, a social process. The quality of the self's interpretation is not simply a product of its own individual effort. The infant and mother (and/or other figures who share the mothering role) together make up a social milieu, an ecology, which shapes a certain cast to the "I am and you are" situation. The later development of partial independence begins to shift more of the interpretive task onto the developing self. But even into adulthood, the basis for interpretation of the meaning of existence remains fundamentally social.

Simultaneously with this social process of early self-differentiation there begins another aspect of the beginning of selfhood, "the psyche indwelling the soma." The body becomes the dwelling place of the self, and a sense of being *in* the body and living *with* another or others takes form. Winnicott's term for this process is "personalisation."[8]

One further concept comes to us from the work of D. W. Winnicott which is of considerable psychological importance as a connecting link to a hermeneutical theory. This is the formulation of the transitional object. The term derives from Winnicott's effort to understand the process by which internal, fantasied object images are connected to external reality. Winnicott speaks of this intermediate object as the transitional object. His particular interest in the mental life of infants led him to focus his attention on the common childhood phenomena of the favorite toy, such as a teddy bear, and the imaginary "friend" of the young child. The transitional object dwells somewhere between fantasy and reality, partially under the control of the self and partially separate and under the control of the environment.

> Of every individual who has reached to the stage of being a unit with a limiting membrane and an outside and an inside, it can be said that there is an *inner reality* to that individual, an inner world what can be rich or poor and can be at peace or in a state of war. This helps, but is it enough?
>
> My claim is that if there is a need for this double statement, there is also need for a triple one: the third part of the life of a human being, a part we cannot ignore, is an intermediate area of *experiencing,* to which inner reality and external life both contribute. It is an area that is not challenged, because no claim is made on its behalf except that it shall be a resting-place for the individual engaged in the human task of keeping inner and outer reality separate yet interrelated.[9]

Winnicott believed that the growing infant is able to negotiate his or her way between imaginary, wishful fantasy and the otherness of reality by means of transitional objects and transitional behavior. Here we see how the self, in its growing need to maintain control of the line of existence, combines imagination and reality perception to develop a certain narrative intermediate space within which an interpretive process can begin to be formed.

In an important book based upon Winnicott's concept of the transitional object, Anna-Maria Rizzuto, a psychiatrist, has proposed that one aspect of the transitional mental life of the developing child in Western culture is the formation of a primitive image of God. Though her work is based on a limited sample of seriously emotionally disturbed individuals, she strikingly documents the way in which such nascent images of God are intimately involved in the living experience of the child and assist the individual in managing the developmental stresses of emerging life. These transitional "Gods" are clearly interpretations based upon the quality of the child's early object relations experience. We might consider them private mythical images that, like the deep cultural myths upon which the great religions are based, emerge from the crucible of life experience.[10]

Like Rizzuto, pastoral counselors are interested in the particularity of the individual experience of God in relation to the deep issues of personal life. These particularities always involve a peculiar mixture of the cultural and faith community images of how God relates to persons and private, idiosyncratic notions that stem from the developmental process. The mythic images of the religious culture to which the individual has been exposed mix freely with the fantasy images that stem from personal experience to form transitional images of God. Out of that mix emerge what might be called private myths of the self's past and continuing relationship with God in the ongoing process of life. If the pastor is to relate to the individual as a representative of the transforming power of the gospel, it is to these private myths of the self and self-God relationship that he or she must relate. As Boisen's living human document image suggests, that task becomes fundamentally a hermeneutical one.

Before moving on to other developments in object relations theory, one final concept of D. W. Winnicott is important for our consideration. This is his formulation of the idea of the true and false selves. If the relationship of the mothering person to the infant is "good enough," the child is able, as he or she moves through the three stages of absolute and relative dependence and relative independence, to develop a true sense of his or her own powers in relation to the true power and authority of the object world. The line of continuity of existence for the self "rings true," is rightly balanced.

However, particularly if the mothering is not "good enough"— that is, if the mothering person(s) insists from very early that the infant conform to the mother's narcissistic need rather than conforming herself to the infant's—a false sense of self may be established.

> Periodically the infant's gesture gives expression to a spontaneous impulse; the source of the gesture is the True Self, and the gesture indicates the existence of a potential True Self. . . .
>
> The good-enough mother meets the omnipotence of the infant and to some extent makes sense of it. She does this repeatedly. A True Self begins to have life, through the strength given to the infant's weak ego by the mother's implementation of the infant's omnipotent expressions.
>
> The mother who is not good enough is not able to implement the infant's omnipotence, and so she repeatedly fails to meet the infant gesture; instead she substitutes her own gesture which is to be given sense by the compliance of the infant. This compliance on the part of the infant is the earliest stage of the False Self, and belongs to the mother's inability to sense her infant's needs.[11]

Here we glimpse again the earliest social beginnings of the interpretive process that sets a direction for a later style of self and interpretation mode of being. The mother's interpretation of the infant's gesture is as important as the infant's beginning interpretation of the situation in which he or she finds him or herself. The eventual outcome of the development of the False Self is a person who seems so to have built up a facade of conformities to his or her social milieu or to the desires and needs of important figures in his or her life that True Selfhood—who one would be if left to one's own judgments—seems obscured or nonexistent. Development shaped by too complete compliance of the mothering object to the infant's narcissism, on the other hand, results in the formation of persons who so insist that the world of relationships conform to their own narcissistic construction of it that they seem totally unrelated or so narcissistically related that their interpretations of the self-world relationship is alienated and equally false. Truth in relationships has its psychological origins in the good-enough truth of the earliest relationships of care in which self and other needs are somehow balanced.

It is right at this point that Winnicott's object relations theory supports a theological judgment that needs to be made on the idolatry of the self found in much of the psychotherapeutic preoccupation with such value-laden concepts as autonomy and self-actualization or individuation. From Winnicott's perspective, individuation is not a process of the individual becoming autonomous and self-sufficient, as much of the popular psychology of our time and, indeed, much of the psychotherapeutic enterprise itself would seem to indicate. Truth and falsehood in selfhood have to do with right relationship, which is able to balance the needs and gestures of the self with appropriate acknowledgment and engagement of the otherness of a reality that does not conform to our wishes. Winnicott's psychological analysis of early infant-mother relationships suggests that it is in a crucible of a degree of suffering and sacrifice on the part of both mother and infant that such right relationships are born. Here we find a very different paradigmatic image from that of the humanistic psychologists who speak of a core of human potential that only needs right nurture and gratification to grow into an autonomous, self-actualized being. Rather we see here a relational paradigm in which suffering, sacrifice, and a certain conflict of omnipotent autonomies play significant roles.

Having found in the writing of D. W. Winnicott the several psychological anchor points to which we may attach our hermeneutical theory, we turn now more briefly to another object relations theorist, the contemporary American Otto Kernberg. The tie I wish to make to Kernberg's thought is a limited one, though readers who wish to do so may find a more thoroughgoing appropriation of his thought useful.[12]

Trained in classical Freudian psychoanalytic theory, including the more recent developments in ego psychology to which I have referred earlier in this chapter, Kernberg developed his theory of the earliest formation of object relations on the basis of Freudian drive conflict theory, making use of such familiar Freudian concepts as introjection, projection, and the like. His particular clinical concern is to develop a conceptual framework for understanding what has come to be called the "borderline" personality. The borderline personality is one who lives on the borderline between psychosis and normality (or neurotic personality organization). Characterized by a tendency to become agitated and depressed, often addicted to various substance abuses or eating problems, and experiencing great difficulty in maintaining stable interpersonal relationships, these persons seem often to experience polarized feeling states and eruptions of alternating rage and hostility and self-denigration. It is often noted that borderline disorders are increasingly found in the population seeking psychotherapeutic help in our society.

Kernberg's contribution to our project comes primarily at two points: his analysis of the way in which positive and negative emotional valences become attached to self and object images to form what we would term positively and negatively valenced interpretations, and the resulting formation of what Kernberg calls splits in the self and object images. Kernberg proposes both of these theoretical constructs for the first twenty-four months of life, most particularly from the sixth to twenty-fourth month.

Like Winnicott, Kernberg conceives of the neonate as experiencing only separate moments of either comfort and pleasure or discomfort, anxiety, and pain. The contradiction of these two dialectically opposed experiences presents the first dilemma to the developing infant. Kernberg calls these discrete moments "all good" and "all bad" experiences.

Gradually these all good and all bad experiences begin to be identified with the same object, the mother, though in a manner that at first identifies her not as the same, but as separate and discrete as the two positive and negative experiences. She becomes somehow the "good" mother and the "bad" mother, an object image split to fit the polarity of early experience.

Concurrent with this beginning object image split, a similar process is going on in the infant's beginning formation of a sense of self. Still fused with the object world, two nascent ego states emerge taking the form of the "all good" and "all bad," as in the case with the mother. All this takes place before the child has a firm sense of the continuity of experience. However, much as Winnicott proposed, Kernberg sees a continuity of existence as a self beginning in the first few months of life. Still fused in the symbiosis of self-object images, the dialectical split now begins to take the form of the "all good mother and the all good me," on the one hand, and the "all bad mother and the all bad me," on the other.

With the coming of a developing sense of the continuity of objects and of self, a critical point of self and object relations development arrives. The experience of the mother and the experience of the self must be separated. Individuation must begin its work. Not only that, positively and negatively valenced experiences must be somehow integrated. Mother (and other mothering figures) must begin to be seen as both good and bad (good enough?), and the self must begin to be seen as neither all good nor all bad, but as an integrated mixture.

> The fusion of positive and negative introjections implies a fusion and concomitant modification of their affect components. The irradiating effect of purely positive and purely negative affective states diminishes. . . . This development, essential for normal psychic growth, also triggers off an additional development of the intrapsychic life: the image of an *ideal self* representing the striving for reparation of guilt and for the reestablishment of an ideal, positive relationship between the self and object. The image of an *ideal object* which represents the unharmed, all-loving, all-forgiving object completes the picture.[13]

Here we see Kernberg's formulation of the integrative interpretive process that must take place if the self is to develop in ways that retain a realistic, bipolar sense of self and of the significant objects in its world. But some persons are unable to achieve this state of integration of the positively and negatively valenced experiences of self and object. A state of being that retains splits of good and bad becomes a more or less permanent style of accounting for the dialectics inherent in all object relationships. The split now takes on, however, a vertical rather than a horizontal orientation. Rather than the horizontal separation between self and object world, the all good self image remains fused with the all good object image and the all bad self image with the all bad object image. In this unintegrated state, the life of the self in its relations with others remains subject to powerful swings between the positive and negative poles of self and other accusation, hostility, and guilt, on the one hand, and grandiose assumption of self and other fusion of interests and gratification, on the other.

As with Winnicott's theory, the pastoral counselor may readily reflect on several possible symbolic connecting points between theology and Kernberg's psychology. For Kernberg the human situation as presented to the neonate is primordially fraught with both good and evil, pain and pleasure. The confrontation with and integration of that situation into a narrative sense of self and object world is the first human task. A kind of story or mythic picture of self and world must be undertaken that incorporates the polarity of what is experienced. As with Winnicott, that is fundamentally a social process as well as a self project. Through his formulation of the concepts of ideal self and ideal object, Kernberg opens the way to a rich and powerful psychological connection between the beginnings of the self's formation of ideals and the images of the normatively ideal in religious communities of faith and life.

It is just at this point of consideration of the notion of ideal self and ideal object that the work of another American, Heinz Kohut, makes an important contribution to our search for psychological connections. Kohut is not usually considered to be closely related to other object relations theorists. He has done his work independently, though, like Kernberg, he has been primarily concerned with understanding borderline personalities or persons with primary problems related to narcissism in his clinical practice. He is much more concerned than is either Winnicott or Kernberg with the influence of changing social values and shifting cultural images on the process of formation of the self.

Kohut is in many respects a classical Freudian. He accepts with certain modifications the Freudian drive conflict theory with its metapsychological constructs of the structures of the drives, ego, id, and superego. This psychology he finds adequate for the explanation and therapeutic treatment of what Kohut refers to as "Guilty Man," the person suffering primarily from internal conflicts.[14]

But Kohut, like Winnicott and Kernberg, is concerned to understand the etiology of human ills that seem to have their origin prior to the Oedipal development of drive conflicts: the problems of the fragmented self. Somewhat like Winnicott, Kohut posits a "nuclear self" that develops out of the earliest relationship with the mothering figure(s). Also like Winnicott, Kohut considers the infant in its own inner experience to be at first symbiotically joined with the world of environmental objects. The first images of the self are, therefore, "self-objects." It is only with the passage of time and, more importantly, with the "mirroring" experience provided by the mother in which the infant's narcissistic need for acknowledgment and confirmation is gratified that the nuclear self becomes established. Without this stimulating and confirming experience, the nuclear self remains weak and ill-defined, ill-equipped to withstand the inevitable narcissistic injuries that human development brings.

Though he disclaims any expertise as a social analyst, Kohut finds connecting links between his work and a number of creative thinkers in the arts and literature who have depicted late-twentieth-century life as alienated and fragmentary. He proposes that, whereas the culture of Freud's time was overly intimate and erotically stimulating while conflicted over sexuality, today Western culture has produced social and familial contexts that are barren of mirroring stimulation and affirmation of the self's value.[15] This changed situation has produced a need for a psychology to supplement drive conflict theory, a psychology Kohut terms a psychology of "Tragic Man" as contrasted to "Self-expressive or Creative Man."[16]

Here we see Kohut proposing a psychological theory for the person who has been unable to write a coherent, creative "story" or coherent mythic image of the self that provides that narrative quality to the ongoing process of day-to-day experience which gives it meaning and a centered self around which a structure of life and management of conflict can be maintained.

> If we turn from theoretical formulation to actual experience, we can say that the healthy person derives his sense of oneness and sameness along the time axis from two sources: one superficial, the other deep. The superficial one belongs to the ability—an important and distinguishing intellectual faculty of man—to take the historical stance: to recognize himself in his recalled past and to project himself into an imagined future. But this is not enough. Clearly, if the other, the deeper source of our sense of abiding sameness dries up, then all our efforts to reunite the fragments of our self with a *Remembrance of Things Past* will fail.[17]

In his reference to the *Remembrance of Things Past*, Kohut is, of course, referring to the monumental work of the novelist,

M. Proust. He is here concerned with the healing of the "discontinuity of the self."[18] The deep source of the individual's sense of continuity is, for Kohut, the nuclear self, a core structure first formed out of early psychic process made possible by the mirroring experience with the mothering object.

> This structure is the basis for our sense of being an independent center of initiative and perception, integrated with our most central ambitions and ideals and with our experience that our body and mind form a unit in space and a continuum in time. This coherence and enduring psychic configuration, in connection with a correlated set of talents and skills that it attracts to itself or that develops in response to the ambitions and ideals of the nuclear self, forms the central sector of the personality.[19]

Kohut's nuclear self is a "bipolar self." From very early, through the process that arises out of the matrix of mirroring and the formation of idealized self-objects (still experienced in symbiotic relationship to the mother) the nuclear self begins to form desires, ambitions, potentialities. These form one pole of the bipolar self. The other pole is made up of ideals, those idealized images of self and world. The developing life of the nuclear self, its sense of coherence and continuity, reflects the manner in which these two poles are held in tension and creatively integrated.

From Kohut's work we derive another psychological correlate to the hermeneutical image of the life of the self taken from Anton Boisen. The life of the self forms an interpretation, a narrative story whose central task is to hold in coherence and continuity the relationships of the self within itself and with the object world beyond. I shall call this work of the self's life the hermeneutics of the self or, in more traditional theological language, the life of the soul, a construct to be developed fully in the next chapter. It is this life to which the pastoral counselor is called and privileged to attend.

My use here of the terms "hermeneutics of the self" and "life of the soul" turns our attention back toward the necessity of correlating what we have gained from the psychological theoretical explorations of this chapter with the theological and hermeneutical work of earlier chapters. The question remains before us: How can psychological theory and theological formulation be interwoven to produce a coherent theory of pastoral counseling?

I have focused our engagement of psychological theory at the point of the earliest beginnings of the sense of self and relationships to the primary others of that period. That focus can, of course, be expanded. Later psychological development—particularly if seen in the manner proposed by such ego psychologists as Erik H. Erikson, who schematizes the entire human life cycle as made up of a series of epigenetic developmental dilemmas—continues to present the self with new situations requiring new interpretations, reformation of the identity, and restructuring of object relationships.[20]

By narrowing our focus to the early beginnings of life, I have planted our psychological anchoring points at the deepest level. Thereby we have seen how the self from the beginning of life is presented with the necessity of interpreting the gap that forms between self and other, self and world. Before there is language, this new situation must be given interpretation. Fantasy, the work of human imagination, provides the self's bridge to the world. But that bridging effort must be met by a caring relational response that is "good enough" both to mirror or support the infant's narcissistic effort to create a world in which it has a place and to assert the caring one's essential otherness.

From a theological perspective we in pastoral counseling will wish to extend the boundaries of this relational crucible out of which the hermeneutics of the self are born and within which they are rightly sustained. Theologically speaking, I would posit a fundamental analogy between the relationship of the neonate to the mothering person and the relationship to God.

Psychologically, the self has its beginnings in the symbiosis with the mother. The fetus literally begins its life within the mother's body, attached to her, yet from the beginning separate. As a neonate that attachment, no longer a physical connection, must become relational—a shift the infant is not able to achieve by itself. The transition must be facilitated by the mother, who, by her sensitive monitoring of the changing needs of the neonate, both adapts to her child's needs and gradually asserts her otherness from the child. The mother thus exercises the choice the infant is not yet able to make.

At first glance it would appear that to be the mother necessary for the child's formation of a sense of "I am and I am not mother" a certain flaw or imperfection is desirable, even necessary. In Winnicott's language, the best mother is "good enough" but not perfect.

When viewed theologically, however, the analogy between the relationship of the mother to the newborn and that of God to the created human individual presents a significantly different relational image. Primordially the life of the self is grounded in God. In the biblical creation story, the creation of the human individual is the crowning act of God's creation. God chooses to make humans in God's own image and thereby bestows upon us a separateness from God's self. In no other way could we humans have been granted a sense of ourselves as separate and able to make our own choices out of our own perceptions of the world. Thus God from the time of creation has responded to the human narcissistic need to be separate, even at the cost of great suffering to God as primordial parent. Yet God also asserts an ultimate otherness. God does not so respond to all our human needs that the world is conformed to our wishes. Within the analogy of that image of God, the "good-enough" mother becomes not the mother who is flawed in her perfection, but the mother who best fashions her relationship to her child in the pattern established by God who both respects human need and asserts the otherness involved in relationship.

Thus a gap is formed between the self and the mother as well as the self and God, and this gap must be interpreted. This interpretation comprises the task of the life of the soul as seen theologically as it comprises the task of the self as we have seen it from the psychological perspective of object relations theory. But, as in the analogous relationship with the earthly mother, this task of sustaining the life of the self or soul is not simply an autonomous activity. Rather the life of the soul is facilitated by God, who both asserts otherness and mirrors the deepest longings of the human spirit.

Shifting from a theological perspective to an empirical, psychology of religion one, Winnicott's concept of the transitional object proposes a useful psychological hypothesis as to how, at the level of the self's hermeneutics, the beginnings of the self's self-conscious relationship to God may take place. If Winnicott's proposal, as developed by Anna Maria Rizzuto, is an accurate one, then we are presented with a model for understanding in psychological terms the manner in which the self's interpretive process with relation to God is intertwined with the concomitant interpretation of the self in relation to the primary parenting figures. Psychologically speaking, the earliest understanding of God may indeed take the form of the idealized self-object image. Only further experience with God in the life of the soul may make possible the meliorating work of resymbolization of the God relationship to modify the earliest influence of the child's separation-individuation process.

Otto Kernberg's psychological dialectics of the experience of good and evil by the neonate, together with his understanding of the development of positively and negatively valenced emotional configurations of meaning and feeling are also important concepts that have rich possibilities in the effort to construct a theological and psychological understanding of the life of the soul. At its core the life of the soul involves the self's grappling with good and evil. The passions of the spirit are themselves positively and negatively valenced. So also with Heinz Kohut's dialectics of the ambitions and ideals. From a theological perspective I must only add that the management of these two sets of dialectics in the life of the soul is not simply a self project. The life of the soul is primordially relational and is embedded in a tradition and a community of faith which provide a certain vision concerning both the tensions of good and evil and of human desire and ideal. It is within that tradition and that community that the individual soul finds guidance and warrants for its choices, its balancing of life's dialectical tensions. The pastoral counselor in his or her care of souls comes as a representative of that tradition and community. They provide his or her primary means of identification. Just what that representative role means in the concrete situations of pastoral counseling waits to be elucidated in later chapters.

Having completed what might well be called another hermeneutical detour, this one into pastoral counseling's contemporary grounding in psychological theory, I shall turn our attention in the next chapter to a schematization of the hermeneutics of the self in the life of the soul which draws its images from both psychology and theology. My hope and expectation will be that such a schema will further assist us in forming a truly interdisciplinary hermeneutical theory for pastoral counseling.

The Hermeneutics of the Self and the Life of the Soul

The task of this chapter is at once an integrative one and a task of further development of our core image, the image of the self as interpreter of its own experience: the living human document. Having in the previous three chapters developed in some detail the images of the self that emerge from hermeneutical theory, certain strands of Christian theological tradition, and psycho-analytic object relations theory, we need now to see how these three languages of the self interrelate. My purpose is not to collapse any one or two languages and the perspectives they express into another. The integrity of each as emerging from a different language world must be respected. I will, however, be proposing that the hermeneutical perspective on the life of the self can serve as a connective bridge or mediating language between the languages of theology and psychology. Hermeneutical language thus might be seen as a metalanguage, a language about languages of interpretation. Theology and psychology develop out of different hermeneutics, different modes and levels of interpretation. I have designated the theory of pastoral counseling I am proposing a hermeneutical theory, therefore, simply because I am attempting a theory that maintains connections with both theology and psychology by way of concepts and paradigms that come from hermeneutical theory.

As we begin this integrative phase of the theory development task, it is well that we consider the three terms I have used thus far to designate the human individual: the ego, the self, and the soul. Two temptations should insofar as possible be avoided in the use of these terms. The first temptation is to use them as loosely interchangeable, as if each term referred to the same entity and meant approximately the same thing. The opposite temptation is to consider ego, self, and soul as pointing to three quite separate and discrete entities. This latter is, of course, the tendency found in such psychoanalytic theorists as Heinz Kohut, though he does not make direct use of the language of the soul.

For purposes of our hermeneutical pastoral counseling theory I will consider the term *ego* to be a psychological term best used to point to that core of individual human functioning at which the nexus of forces that shape human conflict come together and are mediated. Ego points to the center of the self when seen from the perspective of dynamic psychology. The ego is subject to the givens of conflicting forces within the individual person as well as the introjected forces coming from the primary relationships.

But the center of the human individual is not simply a nexus of forces. A responding, interpretive core of experiencing being forms the center upon which these forces act—Winnicott's central self or Kohut's nuclear *self*. I would see this central nuclear self not as a separate entity from the ego, but rather as the core of the experiencing human being when viewed through the perspective and language of object relations theory. To use the designation self is to emphasize the line of experienced continuity and interpretive capacity which emerges from the self's object relations. To use the term ego is to emphasize the coming together of a nexus of forces demanding mediation and compromise. Thus, hermeneutically speaking, my use of the two terms will assist us in holding together the two languages of force and of meaning.

The term *soul* is here used as a theological term that points to the self's central core subject to the ego's conflicting forces and to the ultimate origins of the self in God. The soul is the gift of God bestowed upon the individual with the breath of life. It is thus the self, including its ego conflicts, as seen from an ultimate perspective—the perspective of the self as nurtured and sustained in the life of God.

There is a sense in which all three terms—ego, self, and soul—point toward the same entity, the central core of individual human life. They are therefore not separate entities, but one. Yet each term points from a different standpoint, a different language construction toward that same entity. Keeping those standpoints clearly separated while yet holding them in a certain functional unity is one of the primary tasks of the pastoral counselor. Thinking consistently about them in hermeneutical terms—as interpretive constructions, each expressing a related but distinct mode of interpretation—will greatly facilitate that task.

There is another term that has been used with increasing frequency in recent years with reference to a central core of the human individual: the term *identity*. I have referred already to its use by both the ego psychologist Erik Erikson and the theologian Jurgen Moltmann. In psychological circles the term identity has found both popular and technical usage. In popular culture, identity has gained wide usage in response to the pluralistic and privatized social situation of modern life. It designates the self's effort to maintain some level of consistent attitude, vision, and response in what otherwise would be a situation of fragmentation. Erikson's use of the term has a more technical meaning, having to do with a certain configuration of characteristics that provide the self with a sense of continuity and self-sameness through the changing circumstances and altering tasks of the human life cycle. Identity thus for Erikson points to a certain idiosyncratic way in which the individual ego performs its tasks of perceiving, valuing, reasoning, compromising, and choosing. In this psychological usage identity is both an individual human project and something conferred upon the individual by the significant figures in the person's life.

Jurgen Moltmann uses the term identity in a less psychologically technical sense than does Erikson. In Moltmann's concept of the paradoxical identity of the church and of the self he does, however, emphasize the conferred nature of identity. Both identity embedded in history and the eschatological identity are received: the one from the historical circumstances in which human life takes place, and the other from the church's or the individual's participation in the coming kingdom of God. In an interesting way, Moltmann, as in the case of both popular usage and Erikson's ego psychology, likewise emphasizes the importance of context in relation to identity. Human historicity creates a certain givenness of context. For better or worse that context will largely determine who we are. But, speaking theologically, for Moltmann there is another context: the context of the coming into reality of the Kingdom. It is that context that holds forth the transforming possibility for human life, including the life of the self.

For purposes of our hermeneutical pastoral counseling theory, I will be using the term identity in both its psychological and theological meanings largely in relation to its emphasis on conferral and context. The life of the soul is thus seen as having largely to do with the self's struggle with the conferred identity of the self's historical social context and the claiming of that identity conferred upon the self by virtue of its participation in the coming Kingdom.

To some readers this rather extended analysis of the various usages of terms pointing to the central core of human individuality may have seemed unduly detailed. In ordinary speech the terms we have considered may indeed be used casually and with little attention to the language worlds from which they come or their nuanced meanings. But, if pastoral counseling is to be truly an interdisciplinary activity, rather than simply a loose eclecticism, just such care as I have given needs always to be taken, at least in theoretical reflection. Clarity concerning one's orientation toward the work of ministry in pastoral counseling requires clarity of conceptualization and language usage.

Three Approaches to Understanding the Life of the Soul

We need now to turn to the task of extending the paradigmatic image of the self as interpreter beyond the early beginnings of the life of the self I have taken from object relations theory. How does the interpretive task proceed in the course of human development? In what form does the self sustain a line of existence and give it meaning? How are all the dynamic forces that play upon the life of the self contained and given meaning by the self's formation of a consistent pattern of interpretation? How are the hermeneutics of the self to be understood, and in what senses can the hermeneutics of the self be considered integral to the life of the soul seen theologically as the struggle of the self with historicity and the claiming of an eschatological identity?

The first thing that is immediately apparent as we consider these questions is that a great deal that has come to be commonly understood concerning human development generally needs to be in the background of our thinking. Certainly Erik Erikson's seminal work expanding the Freudian developmental paradigm is central to this background. The concept of stages of growth, the dilemmas that accompany those stages, and the virtues or strengths that can result from successful coping with stage-related dilemmas all contribute to a multifaceted picture of the common process of development given unique shape by particular cultures, subgroups within a culture, individual family constellations, and even individuals themselves.[1] Theories of faith and moral development likewise add useful dimensions to background consideration of human development.[2]

When these questions are approached from the standpoint of the hermeneutics of the self and the life of the soul, however, a somewhat different set of considerations moves into the foreground of our attention. Though it is not my intention to be exhaustive, I will take up these considerations under the rubrics of (1) the dialectics of the self's hermeneutics in the life of the soul, (2) the formation and transformation of the self's hermeneutics in the life of the soul in relation to three levels of time, and (3) the narrative quality of the self's hermeneutics in the life of the soul.

We have already seen in the last chapter how the necessity that initiates the infant's interpretive activity emerges from the tensions of the new situation of the self in the world. Needs are increasingly not met immediately. A gap develops between the self and the mothering object. Desire is brought into tension with reality.

As the infant grows into childhood and later into adolescence and adulthood, the tensions between desire and reality, need and limited response to need, and what Kohut has called ambitions and ideals, to name but a few of real life's tensions, become increasingly complex. The necessity and role of the self's interpretation of its situation becomes greater and more complicated. The achievement of language usage and the expansion of the self's object relations beyond those with the mothering object add both to the complexity of the task and to the interpretive possibilities. Interpretation of the meaning of relationships and relational demands and expectations plays a larger and larger role in the maintenance of a sense of self. A certain style of interpretation or hermeneutic by which the self makes its interpretations of the flow of experienced life begins to emerge.

I am not speaking here, of course, of a highly self-conscious, deliberate, and simply intellectual process. Though the individual's cognitive capacities play a significant role, the central core of the self's interpretation of the flow of experience is rooted deeply in the self's affective and imaginative life, the life of symbolism, fantasy, and positive and negative feeling. To extend D. W. Winnicott's language, it is the role of interpretation to sustain and solidify the line of continuing existence that provides the self with a sense of continuity at all levels of its functioning. The line of life becomes a line of interpretation—the hermeneutics of the self. Within a theological perspective I would place that process at the center of the life of the soul in all its relationships. The problem before us, then, is that of conceptualizing how the life of the soul is sustained in the hermeneutics of the self.

The Dialectics of the Self's Hermeneutics

The first rubric by which I will attempt to understand the hermeneutics of selfhood is to propose that the process is a dialectical one: that is to say, the self's hermeneutical task is one of holding in tension or dialectical relationship several poles of force and meaning. Though the self, in its lived life, experiences these dialectics in myriad forms and constantly shifting patterns, for purposes of analysis I will schematize them in a general way as in Figure 1:

Figure 1

The Dialectics of the Life of the Soul

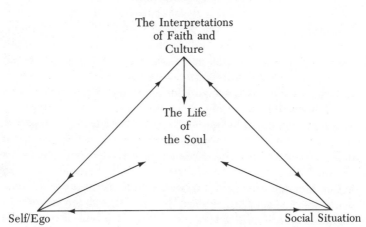

The Interpretations
of Faith and
Culture

The Life
of
the Soul

Self/Ego   Social Situation

In this schema I make use of a spatial metaphor to suggest that the force/meaning nexus that shapes the life of the soul may be seen as coming from three general directions in the life space of the individual. Primary are, of course, those force/meaning configurations that come from the psychological formation of the self and the ego conflicts that emerge in the course of development. These include the bipolar tensions of the self (Kohut), the sedimentations from the early struggles with good and bad self-object images (Kernberg), and the accumulation of ego conflicts (Erikson). I would see each individual as having a certain set or configuration of self and ego issues that provide the core of the life problem of the self in the life of the soul. This configuration shapes a certain disposition and deeply patterned self-object relational stance that is, for the individual, characterological. In the life of the soul this force/meaning vector both poses the individual's most intimate and privately pressing problem and provides the drive and desire necessary for a life in relationship to the world.

A second set of force/meaning configurations enters the life of the soul from the direction of the social context in which the individual is located. Here I have lumped together a wide range of considerations, including the broad sociocultural context (middle-class white or upwardly mobile black America, for example); the more immediate community, work, and extended family context; and the intimate interpersonal context of relationships with those closest to the person. From this direction come the individual's primary relational dilemmas, expectations of commitment, and pressures for conformity to family and group norms of interpretation and behavior. Primary conferral of identity and patterning of ambitions and ideals originate in the relationships of this force/meaning nexus.

A third configurational force/meaning direction—one that is often neglected by purely psychological or psychotherapeutic analysts of human individual behavior—I have called in Figure 1 the interpretations of faith and culture. From this direction come most particularly those mythic and symbolic interpretive patterns by which a tradition or way of life is shaped over time in a given locale. Meanings that are taken for granted as the way things in the world are or should be are shaped in the ongoing process of faith traditions and cultural history. They not only provide languages by which behaviors and relationships are given meaning, but also exert a powerful force in shaping the individual's perceptions of self and world. They tell us what thoughts and behaviors should be assigned guilty, accusatory meaning and what should receive commendation. They define for us what relationships should be and why. In large part the individual's sense of self and world are bestowed by the interpretations of faith traditions and culture.

It should be apparent from Figure 1 that these three broad directions of force and meaning do not come to the life of the soul as separate, discrete considerations. Thus I have indicated two directional arrows between each of the three force/meaning clusters. This indicates the constant interactional process that makes up the flow of life in which the life of the soul is embedded and nurtured and/or kept in bondage.

Pastoral theologians will notice at once that I have not included the force/meaning power of God's activity or the relationship to God as a separate direction acting upon the life of the soul. The theological reason for this apparent omission is found in my thoroughgoing incarnational approach to theological reflection. The force/meaning nexus of God's activity and relationship is, as we saw in chapter 3, a power that participates in all the force/meaning influences upon the life of the soul. It must be acknowledged, however, that this formulation presents us with an ambiguity and a mystery. God is both wholly other from creation and incarnate within the force/meaning processes within creation. In the trinitarian language concerning God the Christian faith tradition has attempted to hold together that unity and separateness along with that diversity and participation in and through the dynamics and meanings in creation.

I need here to reemphasize that within the schema of Figure 1, the life of the soul is a continuous life of interpretation: a life of attaching meanings to behavior, relationships, the self's maintenance of its line of life, and the intimations of the recurrent conflicts of the ego that press upon the soul's struggle with existence. By its hermeneutical, interpretive process the life of the soul holds together in a dynamic tension a virtual myriad of often conflicting demands, expectations, drives and desires, emotions, relational commitments, meanings and values, perceptual patterns and ways of seeing the world.

I have called this central interpretive process by the dual title "the hermeneutics of the self in the life of the soul" primarily to indicate two things—one psychological, the other theological. From a psychological perspective, taking my original cue from Boisen, I locate the central problem of the self in its hermeneutical process: the connection of experience with ideas and symbols. From a theological perspective I affirm that the life of the soul does not have to do with some isolated "spiritual" relationship to God separate from the life of the self in the world. Rather, the life of the soul in relation to God is part and parcel with the life of the self in all its relationships, its struggle to find integrity at the connecting nexus of a confluence of forces and meanings. This view of the life of the soul assumes a God who is active in the world, incarnate in created life, and purposeful in history.

The Life of the Soul in Relation to Three Levels of Time

The second rubric under which we will consider the hermeneutics of the self in the life of the soul has to do with the experience of the individual in relation to three levels of time: time within the human life cycle, time within the process of human history, and time within the structure of the life of God in relation to creation—eschatological time.

Figure 2 schematizes these three levels of time. For purposes of explication, the schema separates out each level from the others. It should be remembered, however, that human life actually takes place and demands interpretation within all three levels simultaneously. It should also be kept in mind that a given individual may be only relatively aware at a given time of involvement in all three levels. Some persons may indeed live a lifetime with only fleeting awareness of the impingements of Level II on their lives and with virtually no attention given to Level III. Few persons, however, go through life without daily confrontation with time at Level I and at least occasional intimations of Levels II and III.

Level I time is that level about which Erik Erikson and other developmentalists have written so well.[3] In this schema the emphasis has been placed on the function of memory and anticipation in structuring the necessity of a continuous process of interpretation and reinterpretation.

Figure 2

THE LIFE OF THE SOUL AND THREE LEVELS OF TIME

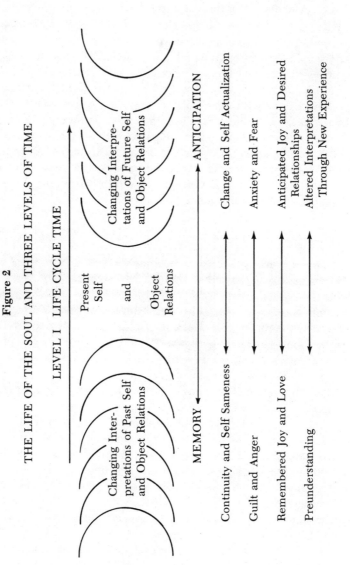

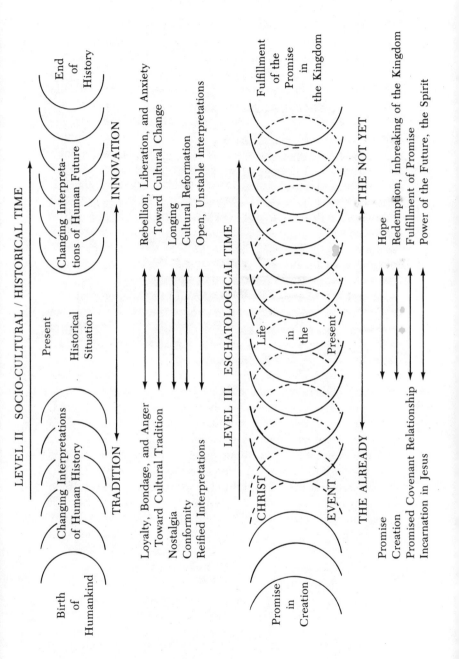

LEVEL II SOCIO-CULTURAL / HISTORICAL TIME

Birth of Humankind

Changing Interpretations of Human History

Present
Historical Situation

Changing Interpretations of Human Future

End of History

TRADITION — INNOVATION

Loyalty, Bondage, and Anger
Toward Cultural Tradition
Nostalgia
Conformity
Reified Interpretations

Rebellion, Liberation, and Anxiety
Toward Cultural Change
Longing
Cultural Reformation
Open, Unstable Interpretations

LEVEL III ESCHATOLOGICAL TIME

Promise in Creation

CHRIST
EVENT

Life in the Present

Fulfillment of the Promise in the Kingdom

THE ALREADY — THE NOT YET

Promise
Creation
Promised Covenant Relationship
Incarnation in Jesus

Hope
Redemption, Inbreaking of the Kingdom
Fulfillment of Promise
Power of the Future, the Spirit

The present moment of experience is always seen as in some sense an extension and continuation of the past. Insofar as that experience has a self reference, it tends to be interpreted as either an incident of fulfillment of the self's past identity, its ambitions, and ideals, or as an interruption of or as discontinuous with the past self. Not only that, the new experience of the present also impinges upon the past interpretations of the self, and its hermeneutical posture, either to confirm or to alter in some way those interpretations. As a matter of fact, looking back over one's past life, it would appear upon reflection that there has been a constant process of interpretation and reinterpretation going on. Who I saw myself to be and who I was in relation to my parents, for example, at age five or ten or twenty were, in memory, quite different interpretive perceptions. From the vantage point of my present age, my self-in-relation at those different ages has yet a different interpretation attached to it—the interpretation given through the perceptive lens shaped by my experience to the present. So it is that the self in its interpretations of both self and object relationships must continually reinterpret within the structure of life cycle time. Events and relationships simply do not have the same meaning when remembered or anticipated at different points within the life cycle.

And yet, paradoxically, present events and at least the earliest events of life do retain something of the same meaning because at the deepest level of unconscious memory, as Freud discovered, individual life cycle time is timeless. Interpretations of life's earlier events and relationships take on a certain forceful meaning such that they act as the meaning templates with which the events and relationships of new experience are to be interpreted. Thus the hermeneutical task of the self in relation to life cycle time includes not simply the reinterpretation of past self-world understanding in the light of new experience, but doing so in a manner that in some way preserves the force of those deepest patterns of meaning. Reinterpretation therefore may be said to involve the transformation of meaning. In theological terms I would see this compulsion to repeat old patterns of self-world interpretation as one facet of what Jurgen Moltmann calls human historical embeddedness.

At the level of life cycle time the human interpretive task is not only retrospective, it also includes the capacity and necessity of anticipation. Life cycle time structures the givenness of the aging process and requires that the self take note of the time in the life cycle that is coming to be. Life cycle time thus flows forward out of the past, but it also flows toward the present out of the future. Thus, if remembered experience carries the weight of continuity and self-sameness, anticipated experience carries the weight of change and self-actualization. Interpretations of past and future provide the linkage between the guilt and anger of the past and the anxiety and fear of the future. Likewise, interpretation links remembered joy and experience of love with anticipated joy and desired relationship. Through interpretation remembered guilts and anger are sometimes linked with desire for more positive relationships in the future as are also remembered love and anxious anticipation.

The outermost boundaries of life cycle time are, of course, the boundaries of birth and death. This means that the hermeneutics of the self must include some interpretive answers to the questions of birth and death. For what purpose was I born? Why and how and when am I to die? The relative urgency of these questions differs at various stages in the human life cycle. The young tend to find the first question more pressing. Aging brings the second more to the fore. Yet, for some, the process comes full circle as in the years of old age they wonder again why they were born. Here we glimpse how the human capacity and desire for self-transcendence drives the self's interpretations beyond the boundaries of life cycle time. Though that level provides the most immediate context for the self's meaning making task, it also presents the urgent requirement for a larger context of meaning to support the self's interpretations.

Individual patterns of interpretation may, to be sure, avoid the whole matter of the questions of birth and death. All pastoral counselors have encountered persons who genuinely seemed to live their lives only in the present moment. Interpretations, when made, seemed only to have to do with present pleasure or pain. Like the object relations theorists, I would see these persons as suffering from the condition of the fragmented, poorly developed self, crippled by the failure of early self-object relations to establish a line of life that has continuity and consistent direction. For these the need is for a relationship that so provides object constancy that a rudimentary sense of self-in-relationship can be established.

The second level of time that sets a boundary structure around the life of the soul is that of sociocultural or historical time. At this level the life of the soul is placed within a given period in the process of human history. To be a self in the latter quarter of the twentieth century structures a very different interpretive task and possibility than was the case for a self in the latter quarter of the first, fifteenth, or nineteenth centuries, for example. Not only is the flow of great events that affect all of the world's cultures vastly different, but likewise the languages, symbols, and cultural interpretive images of our time offer a very different set of socially legitimated interpretive options in which to participate. The social dynamics of a particular sociocultural time and place impinge upon the self and ego processes of the individual in subtle but powerful ways to skew the self's ambitions and ideals in certain ways to conform to the times in which one lives. To the extent that these social dynamics and their interpretive stylistic fashions penetrate to the level of primary object relations (as, for example, did Victorian fashions with regard to sexuality and parental protectiveness) they impinge upon and shape the dynamic forces of the ego.

Here we encounter again the fact of human historical embeddedness. The self does not engage in its hermeneutical process in isolation and privacy, though its experience of the life of the soul may have the aura of private thoughts, secret meanings, and reluctantly shared interpretations. In reality the self's hermeneutical process is, at the level of sociocultural/historical time, a profoundly social process. We are embedded in a virtual ecology of meaning and language that we share with our fellow travelers through the process of historical time.

Figure 2 schematizes the polarities of Level II time in a manner analogous to those of Level I. The continuity of cultural traditions vies with the innovation of cultural change to shape a certain cultural interpretive problematic for life in the present historical situation. Just as history is being constantly rewritten in the light of current cultural imagery, so also are common cultural interpretations of the human future. Loyalty, bondage, and often suppressed anger toward cultural traditions vie with rebellion, liberation, and anxiety concerning cultural change to form a sociocultural dynamic in which the self through its own hermeneutical process must find a place and sense of kinship with others. Nostalgia competes with longing for the new, as does conformity with cultural reformation. In its own hermeneutical process the self must, with greater or less self-conscious intent, develop a style of interpretation that is located somewhere between the poles of reification of cultural interpretive modes and the risks of open, unstable interpretations that may lack social support.

Within the Christian vision there is a third level of time within which human individual life and corporate history is contained: time within the purpose and promise of God. In Figure 2 this level of time is schematized as eschatological time, time as seen from the standpoint of human eschatological identity. This is time measured by the activity of God in relation to creation and the promise of fulfillment of creation in the kingdom of God.

At this level of time the continuities of the past do not simply come into conjunction with the anticipations of the future in the present moment of time's process. Rather, there is a more fundamental and encompassing coming together of past and future time in the event of Jesus as the Christ. In him time at the human historical level and time in the life of God were so merged that a new process was set in motion in time: the time of God's coming into fulfillment of the power and promise made in creation. From that time forward the time of the Kingdom came into history. Life in the present is therefore lived within the *already* of that incarnational coming into history of the power and promise of the Kingdom and the *not yet* of the final fulfillment of that promise and power.[4] To the extent that we humans live our lives participating in the identity bestowed upon us by our life in this level of time we lay claim to the eschatological identity of our life in the life of God.

The dynamic polarities within the level of eschatological time are schematized as the dynamics of the *already* and the *not yet* of the full coming into unity and wholeness of creation in the life of God. They are, on the one hand, the force/meaning dynamisms of God's action in creation, God's promised covenantal relationship with humankind, and God's incarnation in Jesus. These image for us in the present the *already* of eschatological time. On the other hand, because we who are in the present live also in the *not yet* of the fulfillment of the divine purpose and promise, we live in hope of that fulfillment, awaiting our redemption in the in-breaking of the Kingdom. In this *in-between* time we live by the power of the Spirit, which is the Power of the Future. Life at the level of eschatological time thus denotes human life within the ecology of the life of God in relation to all creation as that life is envisioned within the Christian narrative account of God and the world.

The Narrative Structure of the Self's Hermeneutics

The third rubric under which we will consider the hermeneutics of the self in the life of the soul has to do with the narrative quality of the self's hermeneutics. Said very simply, this means that the self maintains its sense of being a self primarily by means of the interpretation of life as a story. Each of us has a story that is "the story of my life." That story embodies in often highly nuanced ways the force/meaning dynamics that make up the dialectics of the self's hermeneutics through the course of all levels of past, present, and future time. Theological ethicist Stanley Hauerwas puts it this way:

> A story, thus, is a narrative account that binds events and agents together in an intelligible pattern. We do not tell stories simply because they provide us a more colorful way to say what can be said in a different way, but because there is no other way we can articulate the richness of intellectual activity—that is, behavior that is purposeful but not necessary. For as any good novelist knows, there is always more involved in any human action than can be said. To tell a story often involves our attempt to make intelligible the muddle of things we have done in order to have a self.[5]

It is by means of this very private and particular, to a degree unconscious or preconscious, story of an individual's life that the self maintains its continuing interpretation and reinterpretation of itself in relation to the world. Because in unconscious ways it retains the self's connections to even the earliest experiences of life, the self's story has about it an aura of a deep myth that images the way things are and should be for that self. Thus the self's story may be seen as the soul's myth of the self in the world.

Like a classic novel or a cultural mythic story, the individual self narrative contains, often in highly symbolic form, representations of the deep forces that interplay in the life of the soul. Psychologically, these forces can, given careful analytic attention, be identified as the dynamic forces of the ego, as well as the polarized forces of the self's ambitions and ideals. At another level representations of equally deep and subtle sociocultural forces may be also recognized and identified by the listener to the narrative whose ears are tuned to hear that level of dynamic.

The deep mythic stories of the individual soul do not, however, embody only the force dynamics that have shaped and continue to shape the life of the soul. They also embody the often conflicted and ambivalent meanings that have interplayed in the self's interpretive process. Such stories present with varying degrees of subtlety the characterizations that have been attached by the self to the most significant figures in the individual's life. Likewise, the self's own self-characterizations, the often contradictory images of the self-in-relation that have developed over time, are given expression in the mythic stories of the soul.

Wesley A. Kort has proposed that all narratives contain at least the following elements: setting or atmosphere, plot, character, and tone.[6]

Setting or atmosphere (Kort prefers the latter term) refers to the whole range of conditions, possibilities, and powers that make up the givens of the situation in which the story takes place. They originate in some power or reified meaning "beyond the borders of human alteration, understanding, or control."[7] Atmosphere may include not only time and place boundaries, but also the givenness of certain values or expected behaviors, violation of which may be expected to bring guilt or blame. Atmosphere is thus the situation as given which must be accepted as presented.

The pastoral counselor who listens to a life story with an ear tuned for atmosphere will immediately be impressed with the force and variety of taken-for-granted meanings. If one listens closely enough one begins to pick up intimations of a certain emotional atmosphere as well. For some the atmosphere will be one of disappointment and continuing hurt, as if the person had been cheated or had essential ingredients for living withheld. For another the atmosphere crackles with latent anger and resentment; for yet another, shame and self-negation. Still further listening may disclose a counter atmosphere that speaks of pride, ambition, or even self omnipotence over all limiting forces. All these aspects of emotional atmosphere speak in some way of the emotional climate in which the individual has lived—an atmosphere that has either been supportive of the person's life and growth or has in some respect been inhibitory or debilitating. In either case the emotional atmosphere will appear to the observer to have been taken for granted.

Self stories may frequently be found to express in more hidden ways an ultimate level of assumed atmosphere that reveals the individual's perception of the final context in which the life of the soul takes place. For some that atmosphere is assumed to be fundamentally friendly toward the self, faithful in its trustworthiness, and accepting of human frailty. For others the final climate of things is more over against the self's intentions or indifferent to the struggles of the soul.

Like all narratives, the story of the self or deep myth of the soul has a plot that embodies a sense of beginnings, a continuing story line, and a more or less problematic ending. Careful listening will virtually always reveal that life story plots are layered with the changing interpretations of the self's history of experience. Asked when a certain story line or self-image began to take shape, persons will often recall a certain incident or time in the past as the beginning time. Further exploration of less readily recalled experience may, however, reveal a much earlier time when the plot of the story began to take its shape, carrying with it certain long forgotten meanings and subtly conflicting symbolic events. Life stories very often also have two conflicting plots, each vying for dominance as the story of a life. Beggars who turn out to be princes in disguise appear not only in classic fiction; the life story of defeat may contain a counter plot that, often in twisted ways, projects victory over one's tormentors. Most particularly, life story plots humanize time by changing the simple sequence of events into experience that has significance and direction. To lose the sense of story line in one's life is to lose the sense of being a self.

The third element of narrative is character. In the listening process of pastoral counseling this element is perhaps the most difficult to uncover or comprehend. It is also the most fascinating for the pastor who resists the temptations of stereotyping and/or diagnostic labeling. Character in life story refers both to the individual's own self-characterization and the characterizations assigned to significant persons in the life story. Characterization is the product of both imagination and behavioral profile. It is both revealed in the events of past and present and imagined in the selective process of symbolization in relation to both self and other. Nowhere is the self's interpretive function more active than in the development of characterization. In the deep recesses of the soul mythic images of the self compete for dominance and mythic images of significant others interact with the images of the self to form the interpersonal templates with which the self interprets relationships, old and new. Likewise do characterizations of God as all-powerful and judging, distant and uncaring, or close and responsive to human suffering take shape through the hermeneutics of the self's interpretations of the ultimately ideal self-object.

The fourth element of narrative, which becomes exceedingly important as a diagnostic and prognostic indicator in pastoral counseling, Wesley Kort refers to as tone. Tone suggests the quality of stance or standpoint from which the narrative is related.

> Tone . . . has three aspects: selection of material, language choice, and attitude—attitude in both a physical and emotional-intellectual sense. The writer chooses to tell us about something, he uses a kind of language or uses language in a certain way, and he has or assumes a certain attitude or set of attitudes toward what he is telling the reader. Now, of course, these three aspects of tone are not separate things; they are together in one act.[8]

The pastoral listener to life stories must give close attention to all three of these aspects of tone. In its interpretive process the self engages in selective attention and inattention to the flow of events and relationships. Habitual patterns of tending to life experience in certain ways develop over time so that given modes of interpretation are reinforced and other possible interpretations overlooked or negated. The pastoral listener soon learns always to wonder why this particular story of experience has been chosen to be related. What is being left out and why? The selective process has created a certain tone for the story. So also with language. Is the language chosen the language of blame and accusation? Is it rather the language of weakness and helpless victimization? Or rather is the language expressive of a determined battle against odds? Some life stories are told in the genre of tragedy; plot and tone speak of the inevitability of unhappy endings and losing battles. Others are told more as a comedy of joys and sorrows, foibles and follies, but with the conveyed expectation of a good outcome. Saga, romance, confession, or merely documentary account characterize the tone of still other narratives of individual myths of the soul.

Emotional and intellectual tone are of equal importance to material and language selection. Some life stories are told in resentment, anger, and suppressed rage; others convey shame, guilt, and self-denigration. Often conflicting emotional tones interplay in ways that hint of ambivalent relationships and hope doing battle with despair.

Pastoral listeners learn to give close attention to changing tones of reports of life experience in the course of a counseling relationship. When such changes occur in consistent and subtly positive ways, they are often the earliest and most reliable indicators of positive change in the life of the soul. The opposite is, of course, true as well. Changes in tone that move consistently in a negative direction indicate the possibility of malignant changes in the life of the self that spell danger and destructive shifts in the force/meaning dynamics.

The foregoing reflections on the elments of narrative in life stories bring to a conclusion my presentation of a prolegomena to an interdisciplinary theory underlying the hermeneutical approach to pastoral counseling. I have drawn from a wide range of materials in theology, psychological object relations theory, philosophical hermeneutics, and, finally, even literary criticism. My choice of materials from each of these fields has, of necessity, been highly selective, leaving as a result a number of problems and secondary issues to be resolved by further work. I hope, however, that I have established the basis for an image of the self as interpreter of its own experience and of the life of the soul as that arena in which the self's interpretive process must find whatever resolution is possible to the force/meaning dynamics of human existence in the context of its life in God.

Having laid the groundwork for the theory, I turn now to the methodological problems of its application in pastoral counseling. Readers who have grown impatient for more concrete clinical data against which to examine the theory's applicability will, I hope, find in Part II some examples of what they have been seeking. The style of the presentation will, however, continue to be that of the unfolding of the formation of a theory rather than that of a case book. Our attention now turns in a methodological direction focused on the possibilities and problems that appear when pastoral counseling is imaged as a hermeneutical process—a process of interpretation and reinterpretation of the hermeneutics of the self in the life of the soul.

Hermeneutics and Pastoral Counseling

Evoking the Story
in the Stories
of the Self

As I sit in my study thinking about the task of this chapter, my mind wanders over countless memories of times when I have sat with a person for the first time to hear a story about something troubling the individual. How often these persons began by indicating that they hardly knew where to begin. My suggestion to begin wherever it seemed right or wherever it seemed easiest rarely made the telling easier. Sometimes it was as if there were so many connections and side tracks that the person was unable to select what was important to tell. Often the beginning was with a question about the self; occasionally it was a question about another person whose behavior had become a source of pain to the teller. Not uncommonly, the beginning story was not the story they came to tell, but another story less painful, less embarrassing, or seemingly less revealing. At times the person, having decided to seek help, came to the moment of disclosure and was inarticulate. But always there were stories—angry stories, sad stories, stories of disappointment and hurt, stories of sensed failure and success, stories of tangled relationships.

Musing about all these stories with which persons have begun a counseling relationship, I find myself thinking of two things all these situations had in common. First, all the stories told in some way of frustrated desire to move ahead with the story of a life. In every case there was a sense of blockage, as if the way ahead in an imaginary plot for the person's life were obstructed. The flow of a life had encountered an obstacle or was being impeded in some way. The nature of the obstruction or impediment varied enormously, but the sense of blockage seems universal among the persons with whom I have had a significant counseling relationship.

Reflecting on this commonality among my memories of counseling beginnings, I am reminded of something I have read concerning the hermeneutical question. It is when the way ahead is blocked that the hermeneutical question is or must be asked. When the processes of life are moving ahead unimpeded, the question as to how we are making sense of things does not press itself upon us. The hermeneutical question arises when the line of life is blocked. If this is so, then we may venture to say that one thing all persons who seek pastoral counseling have in common is that they are asking a basic hermeneutical question—a question concerning their interpretation of the meaning of things. Not that everyone who seeks a pastoral counselor is self-consciously asking a question about interpretation. No, the degree of self-awareness about that varies enormously. Rather, I am suggesting that implicit in every story beginning a counseling relationship there is a hermeneutical question. "What does it mean?"

The second thing that I am aware of as I reflect on the beginnings of my past counseling relationships is that in each case what was going on in my head as I listened to the presenting stories could best be described as a search for the story of the person's life that I assumed was hidden in or lay behind or beneath the story being told. My search was for a narrative story line that I could identify as the central narrative account of a life. If I could get a sense, albeit at first an intuitive one, of the story of the self to whom I was relating, I could gain a toehold on an appropriate answer to the question of my response to the person. My own hermeneutical question—the question as to how I was to interpret what was being said to me—could begin to be answered only as I began to get a sense of the narrative within the presenting stories. Not only that, but also I could then begin to interpret the nonverbal signals—gestures, facial expressions, posture, feeling tone, and so forth—that I was receiving from the person.

What this second reflection on my beginning counseling memories suggests is that there is a certain correspondence between the narrative quality of the self's hermeneutics and the first hermeneutical task of the counselor. Just as the individual self maintains its sense of being a self by means of a narrative or multilayered self story, so also the beginning phase of pastoral counseling is concerned with listening for that self story as it is present in the presenting stories of the person seeking help.

Here we must remind ourselves of the analysis of the hermeneutical process given us by Hans-Georg Gadamer referred to in chapter 2. The pastoral counselor does not come to the first encounters with the self stories of the other person empty-handed. He or she comes rather with a certain preunderstanding shaped by the previous hermeneutical process of the counselor's own life, including particularly the residue of understanding from previous counseling experience. Certain signals, verbal and nonverbal, have come to have certain meanings attached to them. To the degree that the pastoral counselor is experienced in counseling, these meanings have become attached to certain formulations of ego conflict dynamics to create a certain preconception of the probable presence of given patterns of conflict dynamics in the presence of given story and relationship themes. Not only that, but also certain prejudices (I use this term here in the nonpejorative sense that Gadamer uses it) as to the presence or absence of significant social dynamics are brought into the mental attention of the counselor. As Gadamer emphasizes, care must be taken to allow these preunderstandings to "play" in the mind of the counselor without their closing off the counselor's attention to the truly new and unique, once-as-never-before qualities of the other's story.

As a matter of fact, these preunderstandings are what make possible the pastoral counselor's giving full attention to the stories of the help seeker with the eyes and ears of one who is attempting to understand. Experienced pastoral counselors, however, learn to make use of these signals of connections between what is being seen and heard and one's preunderstandings not as templates or molds into which to force all new disclosures from the other, but as soft, tentative images of who the other may indeed be. In Gadamer's language, what is sought is not some ahistorical, objectified formulation of the truth about the other person which can then be imposed upon the faulty interpretations of the troubled person as the "facts of the matter" or the true interpretation. Rather, and continuing in the vein of Gadamer's hermeneutical theory, what is sought is a fusion of horizons of understanding such that the counselor is able to enter the force/meaning world of the troubled person—the other's horizon of understanding of his or her life story—that the understanding of both may be enlarged and illuminated. Therein lies the hope that both life stores, that of the help seeker and of the helper, may undergo transformation, though by its nature pastoral counseling will focus primarily on altering the hermeneutics of the self of the one seeking help.

It is through the appropriation of this open-ended perspective on the beginning process of pastoral counseling that the pastor may come to value the inevitable anxiety that a new counseling relationship entails. Such anxiety signals that something truly new and potentially transforming may take place. It is also in these earliest moments of counseling that in my experience I have come to value deeply my appropriation of the Christian trinitarian understanding of the work of the Holy Spirit. In that gap between my own preunderstanding of what I am about as a pastoral counselor—what I hear and see and look for—and the other person with his or her preunderstanding of what the problem is and what is needed, lies the arena in which the Spirit may be expected to be active.

An Example of Beginning Pastoral Counseling

When Susan Clark called me to ask for an appointment she introduced herself as a friend of a former counselee of mine. She said she had been having some "family problems" and felt depressed. Her friend had suggested she call me. I indicated my openness to seeing her "to see if together we can get a better sense of what the problems are and together decide if we think I can be of help." A time was set for our first face-to-face conversation.

In the time prior to that first appointment I found myself thinking about Susan's friend, my former counselee. Her struggle, in which I had participated over a period of a year or so, had been with a deep desire to be on her own. She was married and the mother of two children, but she felt restless and caged. We had uncovered a number of reasons for her restlessness, some circumstantial and some more related to her own history as a "good girl" of helpful parents who had married right after college an equally helpful but somewhat passive husband. The new story for her life that counseling had opened up for her had been an often risky and at times erratic adventure in self-reliance and freedom. At one point she had even left her husband and children for a time. Needless to say, she had gone through some deep struggles with guilt and rebellion. My own role with her had been primarily that of affirming her desire to be a person on her own and of interpretive conversation partner with her as she uncovered some of the entanglements with parents and husband while searching for ways to set her own limits for her life.

All these memories of my prior experience with Susan Clark's friend ran through my mind as I awaited my first face-to-face encounter with Susan. I recall vaguely wondering what the connections might be between the familiar life story of my former counselee and the new story I was about to hear. My predisposition was to expect that the connections would be there. Something in the manner of the telephone conversation had spoken to me of restlessness and frustrated wishes. Yet I wondered if this might simply be my own preconception—a preunderstanding I was bringing to the new relationship as yet hardly begun.

My first impression of Susan Clark was of a fortyish, slightly plump but attractive woman who looked a little frazzled and tired. She began by saying that she really didn't know why she had come; she should be able to deal with things herself. I immediately recognized a familiar theme from my old relationship with Susan's friend: the wish to be on her own coupled with hints of guilt and perhaps resentment at having to depend on someone else. My preunderstanding had received initial confirmation.

"I really don't know what's happening to me! I know I'm not happy. I should be. I have a good job working with people I enjoy. I have two fine children, even if one of them does have to have a special school. My husband—well, we get along OK, but it never has been what I wanted really." Then tears and apologies.

In this brief, tearful statement Susan had given me a number of important clues to the nature of her immediate stress as well as to some possible narrative themes in her life story. She had begun to share her unhappiness, so closely linked to a strong sense of obligation—"I'm not happy. I should be." Was this a deep mythic theme of her life or a more superficial reaction to present stress? My preunderstanding told me that it was probably the former. Her unhappiness and sense of obligation were immediately linked to three important sets of relationships in her life: her co-workers, her children, and, most painfully, her husband. The fact that she mentioned some "special school" need of one of her children caught my ear, and I wondered momentarily if that relationship held some particular "ought" for her. I wondered what "It never has been what I really wanted" meant. That sounded like a longer and more complicated story. I also wondered about the tears; did they hint of a sad and painful life story? Or were they more angry tears of frustration? An appeal? What was the story behind what I was seeing and hearing? Where did I fit in that story, or rather where did coming to me as a *pastoral* counselor fit?

What I am seeking to convey by this sharing of the first moments of a particular pastoral counseling relationship is that the first pastoral diagnostic task in a situation such as my first encounter with Susan Clark is the task of beginning to hear and piece together a coherent narrative that tells the story of the person's life as he or she has interpreted it. It is this narrative that will provide the entrance into the world of the life of the soul of the other person. Rarely, if ever, will that story be told in a straightforward, full, and finished form. Indeed, it may never have been thought, let alone told, by the person as a coherent, structured, and plotted story. Its appearance to the person as well as the hearer will more likely be in fragments, themes, vague connections, and symbolic images. Nevertheless, I can assume that such a narrative exists or is being lived out in the life of the person. It is this story that embodies the self's interpretation of its life. At the center of the story lie the deep issues in the life of the soul of the person.

By the end of my second conversation with Susan Clark the skeletal outlines of the plot of her life story were beginning to manifest themselves. She had by then told me that her work on two jobs, one as a clerical employee in a busy office and the other as a church choir director, was necessitated by her younger child's moderately severe learning disability. Jamey had not been able to keep up with his classmates in first grade and for the past four years had been enrolled in a private special school. The tuition was four hundred dollars a month, and the school was located some twenty-five miles from the Clarks' home in a formerly rural village on the growing edge of the metropolitan area. Susan had secured employment near the school, and her two salaries paid for his tuition and their daily commutation with a little left over to pay for ballet lessons for the Clarks' older child, a bright and precocious daughter, age thirteen.

Work on the two jobs was not hard. Susan enjoyed both the clerical work and her music, the latter being a token extension of a more ambitious vision of a musical career engendered in Susan by her mother from an early age. But the grind of getting up every morning at five, feeding her family, and getting Jamey and herself off to the city by 7:15, coming home to a family of four and then going off to choir rehearsals was heavy and the road ahead at times seemed interminable.

As I heard this part of Susan's story I was struck again with the theme of obligation and desire for freedom. I found Susan's willingness to set for herself this busy schedule of work and care for her children thoroughly admirable, and yet I sensed an underlying tone of resentment that seemed to be attached not so much to the children as to her husband and, somewhat strangely, her mother. The latter came into our conversation very early as Susan was relating the "facts" of her situation. It seemed that Susan's mother and father had visited the Clarks soon after the father's retirement from his job in industry in Detroit some two years ago. The result of that visit was that the parents had decided to move South to get away from the cold winters in Detroit and had bought a house a few blocks from Susan's home "to be near the grandchildren and help out Susan." Grandmother "looked after" Susan's daughter after school, drove her to her ballet lessons, and was available to take care of Jamey if he was sick and had to stay home from school.

Susan's characterization of her mother attracted my attention immediately. It soon became apparent that her relationship with her mother was a central theme in Susan's life. The picture she presented of her mother was of a powerful and dominant woman who had opinions about everything that went on in the Clark household and sought to impose those opinions on everyone, most particularly Susan. Yet mother had always genuinely wanted to be helpful, and her ideas about what should be done were usually right. She sometimes cleaned Susan's house for her when Susan was tired and had even loaned or given the Clarks money when they were short of funds. Her help was truly helpful; yet Susan deeply resented the control she felt her mother had long exercised in her life. Susan's father, too, had been helpful but had not exacted the price of control of her life that Susan felt her mother did. Father loved Jamey, and the two of them could spend hours happily together.

At some point in this recital of Susan's problem with her mother I moved to flesh out a bit that emerging theme with a question about earlier history. Had it always been this way with Susan and mother? That question brought forth some interesting information. Susan was an only and adopted child. Not able to have children of her own, Susan's mother had adopted her as an infant. Little was known of Susan's biological parents, though Susan confessed to having many fantasies about her mother as a child. As with many adopted children, these fantasies were linked to any and all feelings of unhappiness toward her adoptive parents. Where and to whom do I belong? had apparently been a most often vague and background question for Susan that at times of stress became more compelling.

At this point in Susan's story some further aspects of my preunderstanding came to the fore in my awareness. I began to make connections with the whole body of early object relations theory such as that discussed in chapter 4. Was I hearing information that could lead me toward the earliest beginnings of Susan's restless pilgrimage? Was the core issue of her life the issue of an impoverished sense of self going back to very early in her life as an abandoned and adopted child? Was I dealing with a lost soul that had never really had a sense of being at home in the world? I asked Susan if she had any other early memories of her childhood.

The memories that Susan could readily recall of her relationship with her adoptive parents were mixed. She deeply admired and emulated her mother's devotion to family and duty, but said she didn't think she and her mother had ever been emotionally close. "I never wanted her to touch me" (a memory I later corroborated in a conversation with the mother). Mother's ambitions for Susan were, according to Susan, very high. Susan was made to take piano lessons very early in life. Her memories of hated practice sessions with mother standing close by came clearly and painfully. Mother influenced her to major in music at college and planned for her a musical career. Her marriage to her husband had come after she had fled her home to another part of the country to get away from her mother's influence. "I think I married him to keep from going back home."

At this point another link between present situation and past life story came to the fore. Susan began, with considerable anxiety and a vaguely communicated sense of shame, to tell me of her conflict with her mother over "the only real boyfriend I had as a teen-ager." The boy was Catholic, and her mother, a staunch

Lutheran, had objected. A battle was fought which mother had won; the relationship with the boy was terminated.

As I listened to this old story of submission to mother's will I found myself wondering about the selection of this material out of Susan's past for sharing with me. The connection between present situation (mother's close and dominantly helpful presence) and memory of mother's hovering over the piano lessons seemed clear enough. My preunderstanding of a frustrated desire for freedom coupled with dependence was being further confirmed. But the story of the lost boyfriend seemed too angrily and painfully told to have simply been another example of mother's dominance. Had mother been in some way right about that, too?

The connection soon became plain. It seemed that some weeks before her first call to me, Susan had received a surprise telephone call from her long lost admirer. He had been passing through the city on business and, on impulse, had called her from the airport. The result had been two brief romantic encounters in motel rooms on subsequent trips through the city. Now she was receiving daily long distance calls at her office, and tentative plans were in progress for a longer time together at some city between his distant home and Susan's. All this information came from Susan to me with much expression of guilt coupled with a certain air of defiance. "I know I shouldn't even be thinking about such a thing, but I'm tired of being on this treadmill! I want to be free!"

The story of her reunion with the romantic partner of her teens was told simultaneously as the story of an unsatisfactory marriage. Sex had never been satisfactory for Susan with her husband. His touch had become repulsive to her, as had been her mother's as a child. The husband's demands for sex had been met dutifully, but with less and less willingness and frequency, especially in the last few years. I recall wondering if there was a connection between this increase in the marital alienation and the parents' arrival from the North. Sex with her old admirer had, on the other hand, been "simply marvelous." "I know now what I have been missing all these years!" The increasingly familiar theme of conflict between obligation and desire took a new twist in my listening mind!

Other storied references to Susan's husband began to flesh out her characterization of him. He had recently quit an accounting job, which paid a modestly good, but not excellent, salary, in order to take a position in sales that, Susan felt, required of him more aggressive ingenuity than he possessed. Her portrait of her husband was of a sincere and steady, but unexciting person who himself was more dependent both on his own parents and on Susan's than Susan desired. But she had always been able to count on him if she really needed anything, and he always had been "good to the children." I caught here what seemed to be a connection between Susan's perceptions of her husband and her description of her father.

Although I have related only the beginnings of the story of my counseling relationship with Susan Clark, the purpose of this chapter requires that we leave the detailing of that story at that incomplete point. We need now to reflect further on the data of the case, making use of its concrete richness to consider the problem of the pastoral counselor's entry into hermeneutical dialogue with troubled persons such as Susan Clark at the level of the life of the soul.

If we distance ourselves far enough from the immediacy of my first encounters with Susan to reflect on the methodological problems with which I was presented, one of the first issues that emerges can be seen as the issue of "facts" versus "interpretations." How is the pastoral counselor to know what is really going on in Susan's life? And, since we are immediately confronted with the apparent relationship between what is going on now and what had gone on in Susan's past life, how are we to know what really went on then? Are the questions about what is really happening or has happened pertinent, or is our concern simply with what is or has happened *as Susan interprets those events*? Is the purpose of my counseling to correct her interpretations of, for example, the mother's remembered behavior in relation to Susan or, on the other hand, to corroborate and confirm those interpretations? Is a "true interpretation" possible or even necessary? The question of the purpose of pastoral counseling is given specific shape from the earliest beginnings of this relationship.

Seen from a hermeneutical perspective, the data we have at hand concerning Susan Clark's distressed situation emerges as being virtually entirely data colored by her interpretations. The facts of her situation are all facts already layered over by her interpretation of them. The events of her life have been woven into an interpretive web that she now experiences as the hard, given reality of her life. As her counselor, I was presented with the question of the truth or falsehood, correctness or incorrectness of this interpreted reality; and from the earliest moments of the counseling relationship I, too, had to begin formulating an interpretation. My earlier comments about the functioning of my preunderstanding reveal the manner in which these interpretations themselves have a history of experience behind them. The question of true and false interpretation reveals itself as a very slippery one indeed, layered as it is by the history of interpretation of both my counselee and myself.[1]

Pastoral counselors may be drawn in two very different directions in response to this problem, neither of which makes adequate use of the hermeneutical perspective we are bringing to the task. On the one hand, the counselor may be drawn in a quasi-scientific direction—a search for the "true facts of the case." What is and was the mother really like? Is the husband actually as passive and lacking in drive as Susan portrays him? Are there distortions of perception and construal of relationships to fit Susan's picture of things? What really happened during the piano lessons or at the time of Susan's adolescent romance? What really happens between Susan and her husband? "Tell me more about it, so I can make a proper interpretation."

The implicit goal, if this tack is taken, would seem to be the uncovering of factual truth so that a "true interpretation" may be made to "correct" the false or debilitating interpretation with which Susan is burdened. Once facts and interpretation are brought into harmony the persuasive power of a true understanding may be counted on to effect changes in relationship and behavior. This approach may, of course, develop into a very sophisticated and complex search for the inner "facts" concerning the dynamic residues of historical developmental experience. It · may take the form of an archaeological search for hidden memories, forgotten facts, and unconscious forces.

Some pastoral counselors will, on the other hand, be attracted in a quite different direction. The "facts" of the case are seen as quite secondary to the importance of Susan's interpretation of them. What Susan needs is acceptance and affirmation—something that, at least to her mind, she has never really experienced from either mother or husband. This is the tack of Rogerian unconditional positive regard—counseling centered in the counselee without questioning the truth or falsity of her interpretations of

experience. "You feel . . ." "You think . . ." "You desire . . ."
Here the basic trust seems to be in the troubled person's inherent
ability, given the proper accepting atmosphere, to come to the
most nearly true and creative understanding of his or her situation
and the best way to live in that situation in the future.

In the force/meaning language I have adapted from Ricoeur,
these two directions toward which the pastoral counselor may be
attracted may be seen as each emphasizing one pole of that
dialectical tension, the first toward the language of force and the
second toward the language of meaning. The analysis in Part I
would lead me to the position that neither of these two possible
emphases alone will suffice. Pastoral counseling must hold in
continual tension the languages of force and of meaning. They
point to two sides of a single dynamic. True understanding of a
human situation must take account of both force and meaning,
both what happened and is happening, and how what happened is
being interpreted. Methodologically speaking, how does one do
that in the beginning phase of pastoral counseling such as I have
described in the example of Susan Clark?

Let us approach that question by reflecting on the data Susan
has presented to me by the end of our second conversation,
utilizing the rubrics of the hermeneutics of the self in the life of the
soul developed in the previous chapter. We will first, then,
consider what Susan has shared, making use of the triangular
schema of the dialectics of the life of the soul. What tentative
impressions can we intuit or formulate in a softly focused fashion of
the deep issues in the life of Susan Clark's soul when we view them
from the angles of vision of that schema?

Looking at what Susan has shared in these two interviews from
the self/ego nexus vector, we are immediately impressed with the
evidences she has given us of possible long-standing difficulties in
sustaining an adequate sense of self as well as of the possible shape
of her ego conflicts. The hard, forceful reality of her adopted state
has very apparently been a problem for her since early childhood.
Her hints at difficulty with feeling close and secure with her
mother from her earliest memories ("I never wanted her to touch
me") were most striking. I have already spoken of my own
immediate associations with object relations theory at the time
Susan shared this information. The continuing difficulty with
touch by her husband, now complicated by the sexual demands his

touch communicates, speaks strongly of the continuation of unresolved early object relations conflicts and of a peculiar, as yet unclear, fusion of her unconscious relationships to husband and mother. A deep issue having to do with desire for closeness and warmth, coupled with anxiety about relationships with those to whom she is closest, begins to present itself in vague outlines.

There are hints of other possible self/ego conflicts in what Susan has shared thus far. She has revealed herself to be one who struggles deeply with the contradictions of guilt and desire in her life. Though there are sexual overtones to her present experience of that struggle, one senses that this issue permeates other areas of her life: her guilty desire to be free and her guilty self-recrimination over her need to seek help. The issue appears at this point to be not so much one of sexuality as of intimacy, self-expression, and integrity in relationships.

The nexus of forces and meanings that impinge on the life of Susan Clark's soul from the vector of her social situation have been revealed in our two conversations as both powerful and reinforcing of her self/ego conflicts. The daily grind of work, commutation, expense, and sacrifice for her children, coupled with the physical proximity of her parents and her husband's insecure vocational situation, make for a social situation in which Susan is under constant reality pressure. That situation reeks of obligation. In many ways her description of her life as a treadmill is not an inaccurate description. Likewise, the appropriate value, if not necessity, of her parents' assistance in the care of the Clarks' children makes her deep desire to be free of her mother's guiding care all the more difficult to achieve. The cage Susan feels she is in is not all of her own making. Neither is the fact that as a woman in the work force she must work at two jobs to make enough to meet the expenses of special schooling for her son and the commonly expected middle-class niceties of extracurricular education for her daughter all her own doing. Susan is in a genuinely difficult social situation.

From the force/meaning nexus vector I have labeled interpretations of faith and culture we can identify a number of issues that seem, even from our brief encounter, to be taking shape. Most obvious is, of course, Susan's caughtness between the moral values with regard to sexuality and marital fidelity of her upbringing, on the one hand, and the increasingly permissive sexual values of the urban and suburban middle-class culture in which she now lives, on the other. Her guilt about her extramarital relationship is deep and strong, but it is strongly countered by the pervasive ethos of self pleasure and right to happiness of our time. That same ethos also counters Susan's deep-seated devotion to duty and obligation to her family.

Though I do not recall that Susan, in these first conversations with me, made extensive use of God language except when she spoke of her mother's Lutheranism, she did somehow manage to communicate in her manner and emotional tone that the issues with which she struggled had for her an ultimate dimension. When she spoke of her mother's faith and beliefs concerning a God who would find her out if she disobeyed his will, I sensed that it was also to this God that Susan had vowed her allegiance and against whom she wished to rebel in demanding her right to be free.

Viewing the hermeneutics of Susan Clark's self as a whole from the standpoint of its dialectics, several possible deep issues in the life of her soul begin to emerge. I have already alluded to the issue concerning the conflict between desire and obligation. That issue now fleshes out as an issue of both authority for her life and struggle for a well-formed sense of being a self with integrity. This issue appears to stretch deep into Susan's developmental history, but also encompasses her closest present relationships and even perhaps her experienced relationship with God. She seems to be having profound difficulty sustaining these relationships without sacrificing her own relational needs and/or her own integrity. To stay on the dutiful treadmill sacrifices her own needs too greatly; to run away or indulge in an affair sacrifices her integrity.

At the ultimate level this issue of authority and integrity or obligation and desire reveals Susan's ambivalence as to whether her image of God is to be fashioned as a projection of her characterization of mother (caring but controlling, needed but unapproachable), or fantasized as an idealized parental object who gives permission for her desire. As I reflected about this possible split in Susan's image of God, I found myself wondering if perhaps her coming to me referred by my former counselee might have meaning in terms of my possible representation of the idealized parental object God. Her foreknowledge of me included perhaps her awareness that I had supported her friend's desire to be her own person.

What is missing in the image of God that Susan has allowed me to glimpse seems, on reflection, to have two aspects. She has not, it seems, been able to appropriate the biblical image of God as the one in whom her security as a human being can finally rest. Her life in God is too much colored by her life in the shadow of a mother she both needs and fears. Likewise, she has not been able fully to appropriate the biblical image of the God who suffers with us as we struggle to live our lives with integrity. This is not the God of our wishful fantasy, but the God who knows who we are and suffers with us in our efforts to "attain to the stature of the fullness of Christ."

It is important to note that in the diagnostic reflections I have engaged in thus far, the direction I have taken is toward formulating some tentative interpretations of possible deep issues in the life of Susan Clark's soul, rather than toward the formulation of a psychological diagnostic categorization. To be sure, one could begin such a formulation, making use of the appropriate psychological diagnostic categories. Pastoral counselors familiar with psychiatric and psychological nosology will perhaps do that, but, within the hermeneutical perspective, such a procedure seems to have very limited usefulness. My purpose is rather to so pursue a narrative inquiry with Susan that the story of her struggle with life may be evoked in ways that open up the possibility of reinterpretation and new direction.

Reflection on the data of my first two conversations with Susan within the rubric of the three levels of time discussed in chapter 5 reveals a number of aspects of her life story worthy of attention. At the level of life cycle time we are immediately impressed with the manner in which Susan's present self-world understanding remains colored by her early interpretation of her situation as an adopted child. A deep-lying mythic theme of her life continues to be that she is one who does not belong where she is. There is another life somewhere else that is rightly hers—a life in which she would be free, loved, and secure. Her story of her early refusal of mother's touch suggests that this theme, now so strong in her relationships with her husband, her mother, and her paramour, is both historically deep and profoundly determinative of her self-understanding. So, likewise, is the theme of duty and monotony in relation to her life where she is. Her story of the piano lessons and her story of her current treadmill of work and care of family have a similar ring to them. To stay where one is is to stay condemned to monotony, obligation, and duty, as well as to live in the absence of excitement, adventure, and freedom. So goes the mythic interpretive story of Susan's life. One wonders if the arrival of the forties in her life cycle, coinciding as it does with the arrival of her daughter's teen-age years, has not heightened the tension between the fantasied wish for another life and her perception of life where she is.

I have already made reference to the possible social dynamics embodied in Susan's life at the level of sociocultural time. Susan clearly characterizes her mother as "old-fashioned," in terms of social values relative to sexuality and marital fidelity, as well as in terms of the exercise of parental authority and surveillance. Here Susan herself seems somehow caught between the times. She longs for a richly erotic sexual life, yet is unable to respond to comparable desires on her husband's part. The emergent cultural issue relative to the possibility of sexual freedom and exuberance that carries with it the threat of licentiousness translates into a personal issue for Susan relative to her desire to recover what she feels she lost as a teen-ager and her identification of her husband with passivity, dependence on her mother, and monotonous duty. The themes of her life story become entangled with the themes of the story of her times.

I have also already commented on some important issues in Susan's life at the level of eschatological time. Within the language of Figure 2 (chapter 5), we may say that the deep issues of Susan's soul I have thus far enumerated have not sufficiently been placed in the context of the biblical vision of God's life in relation to creation. She has not as yet been able to appropriate her eschatological identity. God's promise for her life remains fragmentary and fantastic. She lacks a rich understanding of the "already" and the "not yet" of the fulfillment of God's promise for her life. She is tempted to make an idol of her fantasied relationship to her paramour, as she is of a life free of obligations to mother and family. Her identity, embedded in her history, still powerfully controls who she sees herself to be.

I trust that it has become clear to the reader that what we have been about in the preceeding several paragraphs is the beginning of what must remain an open-ended formulation of a narrative interpretive story of Susan Clark's life pilgrimage. The distanciation that reflection on the raw data of the first two interviews has provided us has allowed a number of possible thematic issues to come to the fore which may guide my further participation with her in making new and potentially liberating sense of her life. We do not yet have, nor probably will we ever have, a full and final interpretation that can simply be shared or imposed upon Susan. Rather, what we have is a working interpretation or an interpretation in process of formation. That working interpretation can now shape the preunderstanding I am to bring to subsequent conversation with Susan. It begins to suggest a vocabulary of language and response to what she will bring to our talks together.

A dual purpose then begins to emerge for at least the beginning phases of pastoral counseling with Susan, both aspects of which will need to be kept in interacting relationship. From the standpoint of the pastoral counselor as interpreter, one primary aspect of purpose is that of continued interpretive reflection and gathering of further impressions as well as factual data to support or alter, elaborate or add to the understanding we now have of narrative themes and issues in Susan's life story. The other aspect, seen more from the side of Susan's own search for understanding and new direction, has to do with my invitation to her to collaborate with me in moving from simply sharing with me stories about the pains and struggles, the joys and sorrows, of her life toward the articulation of an as yet unspoken narrative story that gathers to itself the deepest issues of her soul's life.

From a hermeneutical perspective my hope and expectation in entering into such a dual purposed search is that in the fusion of horizons of understanding of Susan's life that may emerge between us, something new and creative may take place that will provide a new hermeneutic, a new and transformed story for Susan's future life. From the standpoint of object relations theory (Winnicott), my hope and expectation could be stated as the creation of a certain transitional space within which new possibilities for Susan's self and object relations may be explored. As a Christian pastoral theologian, my hope and expectation may be better stated as the opening of that space in which the work of the Spirit may be facilitated and a new life story rooted in Susan's eschatological identity as a child of God may be appropriated.

Pastoral Counseling's Hermeneutical Circle: a Proposal

Readers familiar with hermeneutical theory will perhaps think it strange that I have not up to this point made use of an important hermeneutical concept, the so-called hermeneutical circle. This concept contains both the hermeneutical understanding of the limits within which any search for understanding or explanation must work, and the possibility of overcoming those limits in a circular movement toward richer and more nearly accurate understanding. Zygmunt Bauman states, in a simple and general way, the concept of the hermeneutical circle: "Understanding means going in circles; rather than a unilinear progress towards better and less vulnerable knowledge, it consists of an endless recapitulation and reassessment of collective memories—ever more voluminous, but always selective."[2]

To follow a hermeneutical methodology in pastoral counseling thus means to commit oneself and subsequently, it is hoped, one's counselee, to a process of indeterminate length. That process includes the sorting over of stories, impressions, recollections, and shared interpretations of relationships with a view to deepening and extending one's own and one's counselee's understanding of the central narrative story of a person's life and the deep issues of that person's soul. The length of time in which this process is undertaken may be as short as a few conversations or as long as a pastoral relationship lasts, with periods of greater or lesser intensity and collaboration. In my own counseling experience I have had both intense and apparently fruitful relationships that consisted of only a few hours together, as well as relationships extending over twenty years or more with intermittent periods of intense work separated by longer periods during which the other person carried on his or her interpretive life unassisted by counseling.

When applied to pastoral counseling, the concept of the hermeneutical circle suggests two possible ways of loosely structuring the flow of conversation, inquiry on the part of the counselor, and construction of interpretive possibilities. The first is most clearly illustrated in my first conversations with Susan Clark. If we examine the flow of those first conversations and my remembered reflections on them, an easily recognizable circular process reveals itself. My initial impressions of Susan as she entered my study and related to me in that first encounter were quickly followed by Susan's references to her present relationships to co-workers and family. In the telling of that story, however, Susan moved to share with me a bit of the history of those relationships (her parents move to a house not far from the Clarks). In the course of that recital I made what, in the context of considering counseling as involving a hermeneutical circle, was a crucial move: I inquired about the earlier history of Susan's relationship with her mother. This led to some further sharing on Susan's part of significant memories about her childhood: her adopted state, her never wanting her mother to touch her, the music lessons. In both my mind and Susan's, a possible connection was established between memories of the past and present relationship dilemmas. The circle then began to move back toward the present, a move that soon included my own attention turning toward the question as to why these particular memories were being shared with me at this particular time in the new relationship between us.

What I am suggesting is that, viewed with attention to the flow of conversation and inquiry, a circular pattern begins to be revealed—a circular pattern that moves from the immediate counseling relationship to the arena of current life relationships to the history of significant relationships, back to the counseling relationship itself. Although the exact pattern will vary somewhat from case to case, I would propose this circular pattern as a typical one for pastoral counseling pursued in the hermeneutical mode. Not to be taken as a prescription for direct questioning on the part of the counselor, it nevertheless may be taken as a softly focused structure for the patterning of pastoral hermeneutical inquiry. If followed informally, but relatively faithfully, it leads toward an ever enlarging, more elaborately nuanced and enriched arena within which greater clarity of interpretation on the part of both counselor and counselee may take place. As Bauman suggests, it is a circular process that indeed could be virtually endless. The richness and detail of human interpretive experience is indeed inexhaustible. The limits placed upon it are arbitrary ones made by the person seeking interpretive help when either the problem that initiated the counseling is resolved or the process seems to have achieved a certain fruition. The pastoral counselor, too, participates in the setting of those limits by virtue of a wide range of goals for counseling, limits of time and energy, and so forth.

Before leaving this particular construction of the hermeneutical circle, one other consideration needs to be mentioned that becomes a rough rule of thumb. Both counselees and counselors can become stuck in one phase of the hermeneutical circle. History can become so fascinating as to become a virtual obsession; likewise can preoccupation with the nuanced meanings of the counseling relationship. The pastoral counseling hermeneutical circle must be kept moving if it is to produce its enriched and enlivened reinterpretive process. The circle, if it is to become a transformative spiral, must keep moving toward larger and larger inclusiveness.

Another possible way of conceiving the pastoral hermeneutical circle, closely related to the three arenas of relationships, but emphasizing more explicitly the human need to evaluate behavior, deserves consideration. This circle entails a process of enlarging the context within which choices—past, present, and future— are made. This form of the hermeneutical circle, while less explicitly illustrated by the case of Susan Clark, nevertheless is implicitly central to the process of those conversations. Most often this circle begins with some evaluative narrative concerning an immediately or a more remotely past action. "I don't know why I called you. I should be able to deal with things myself." As in Susan's case, this evaluative communication may be accompanied by expressions of guilt, shame, positive self-regard, or angry defiance, as the case may be. Soon the circle moves toward some disclosure of the dialectics of the person's choice or behavior. Such disclosure may emphasize internally felt conflict, interpersonal conflict, or perhaps conflict of values at stake in the choice or behavior. A third arena will often emerge from this one: the expression of desire or intention concerning future behavior or choice that carries with it the weight of the person's frustrated longing for change and more positive self-evaluation. A circle of moral reflection and concern is set in motion which, as in the case of Susan Clark, invites the counselor to declare a role or reveal a moral stance in relation to the troubled person. The pastoral counselor is, from the hermeneutical perspective, most helpful when his or her response at any point in the circular process is primarily designed to enlarge or enrich the arena of reflection within which the evaluation of behavioral choices takes place. Here, of course, the elements of the more historical and relational first construction of the pastoral hermeneutical circle I have proposed become important.

Having examined some elements of the hermeneutical approach to beginning pastoral counseling by means of detailed reflection on my early counseling relationship with Susan Clark, we return in the next two chapters to the problem of change in pastoral counseling. Readers should retain much of what we have considered in this chapter as basic methodological concepts for the full process of counseling, whether that process be for a short or extended time period. The notions of enlarged preunderstanding, the possibility of fusion of horizons of understanding, uncovering the deep narrative issues for the life of the soul, and the hermeneutical circle remain at the center of our theory of change, just as they have been in our consideration of beginning counseling.

Changing the Story: Psychoanalytic, Hermeneutical, and Theological Perspectives

In this chapter we once again turn to the central problem that calls pastoral counseling into being, the need and desire of persons who come to the pastoral counselor seeking to change their lives. What do we mean by change in pastoral counseling? How is change to be brought about? What are the limits of change within which the counselor must work and which the help seeking person must come to accept? What methodological resources does the pastoral counselor have to call upon in seeking to facilitate creative changes in persons?

Psychologists and psychologies have developed widely differing points of view concerning this problem, both at the level of the nature and limits of change that is possible and at the level of therapeutic methodology. Behaviorists, with their narrowly scientistic approach to the problem, tend to see change in equally narrow behavioral terms as brought about through the operant conditioning methods of behavior modification. Marriage and family systems and communication psychologies see change in terms of altering arrangements of family structural dynamics and altered communication patterns. Active intervention into the patterns of behavior and relationship structures is seen by therapists utilizing these methodologies as offering the most viable possibilities of effecting change in persons. These methods may be seen, within widely varying theoretical rationales, as each emphasizing a language of force in relation to engendering change. The force of the therapist's persuasion, the prescription of behavioral changes, or the manipulation of the relational forces that surround an individual is pitted against the forces of behavioral and/or relational patterning that are considered to be causing the problem. Thus the therapist takes more or less forceful control of the situation in order to effect desired change. Psychological therapists of these persuasions tend to discount the value and importance of altered understanding of the problems that are causing the stress as either unnecessary or ineffective. Insight (altered understanding of meaning), they say, does not alter behavior and behavior is what determines quality of life.

Some pastoral counselors will be drawn to these behaviorally oriented methodologies because of their perceived pragmatic usefulness. The urgency to solve practical problems of human behavior and relationships gives these methods an apparent advantage over the more time-consuming and seemingly nebulous methodology focused on exploration of narrative history and meaning. Practical problems must indeed be given consideration. The position of this book is, however, that immediate practical problems always have deeper historical roots. Furthermore, my theological concern for a depth understanding and response to the life of the soul will cause me to question the long-term depth implications of an emphasis upon pragmatic and forceful alteration of behavior. If the life of the soul does indeed involve the self's interpretive process within a framework of meaning that relates all aspects of life and relationships to a structure of ultimate meaning grounded in God, then the pastoral counselor as ministering carer of souls will wish to embrace in his or her work only those methodologies that hold forth the possibility of enlarging and enriching that interpretive process. Behavioral approaches to change will be seen as having real but limited usefulness in ministry seen as the care of souls. In certain unusual circumstances they may be necessary to assist persons to break through such blatantly destructive behaviors as alcoholism, child or spouse abuse, and the like.[1]

The psychoanalytic tradition, with which we have been in dialogue earlier in our engagement of object relations theory, has had a more balanced approach to both the understanding of personality change and therapeutic change technique than has behaviorism or family systems theory. As the discussion of Ricoeur's analysis of Freudian theory in chapter 2 indicates, Freud himself vacillated between placing his confidence in change brought about by deepened and enriched insight into unconscious symbolic meanings and the meaningful recovery of repressed memories, on the one hand, and in the alteration of the dynamic force structures of superego, ego, and id, on the other. His often quoted maxim, "Where Id is, there let Ego be," itself contains both the expectation that enlarged conscious ego insight into id dynamics and the alteration of the force balance between ego and id could be expected to bring about the desired changes in personality functioning. In the Freudian tradition the strengthening of ego controls (force) and the deepened insight into dynamic ego conflicts (meaning) have long been seen as virtually synonymous goals for desired changes coming out of psychoanalytically oriented psychotherapy.

Object relations theorists, because of their clinical concern for understanding and giving therapeutic assistance to persons with an impaired sense of self due to early infantile narcissistic injury or individuation failure, have placed their emphasis with regard to change on the formation of integrated self and object images.

> An authentic self can come about only when diverse self-images have been organized into an integrated self-concept, which relates, in turn to integrated object-representations. Therefore, clinically speaking, the road to authenticity is the road to integration of mutually dissociated aspects of the self. There are many patients whose "true self" does not lie hidden under repressive barriers, but exists only as a potential, fragmented structure. This potential structure may become actual only after efforts at integration in the course of a psychotherapeutic relationship.[2]

As an object relations theorist, Otto Kernberg here clearly associates change with integration and wholeness, the development of an authentic "true" selfhood to replace the fragmented and dissociated self images. Altered behavior and relationships cannot take place until the self can achieve a greater degree of integration. The primary goal of a therapeutic relationship is therefore the facilitation of changes in the self in relation to its fragmentation and inauthenticity.

Here comes into view an apparent affinity between therapeutic change as seen by object relations theory and the hermeneutical approach to the care of souls I have been developing. The rubrics under which I discussed the hermeneutics of the self in the life of the soul in chapter 5 all point toward the need for integration and wholeness. The soul that is unable to sustain an integrated sense of wholeness in the midst of the dialectical tension of the force/meaning nexuses I described will experience fragmentation and need for integration. The hermeutics of the self will not hold together; a new structure of meaning must be found. Likewise, the soul unable to integrate its life at all three levels of time will experience alienation, fragmentation, and need for integrating its experience of life in its own life cycle with life in relation to the history of human relationships and its life in God—its eschatological identity. The narrative account of the life of the self must attain a certain wholistic unity so that the various sub-themes and issues in the life of the soul are held together in a unified story of the self. Without such a unified story the self will experience fragmentation and loss of an integrated sense of being a self.

What I have done in developing the hermeneutical theory of the life of the soul is, of course, to greatly enlarge the arena of integrative concern from the more limited self psychology of object relations theory, while at the same time retaining the object relations viewpoint with regard to the developmental process by which the early nuclear self takes form. The arena of potential fragmentation is enlarged to include all aspects of the self's interpretive life, including the ultimate aspect of its life in God. A larger view of the wholism to be sought in the pilgrimage of the life of the soul is the result. It is not simply the wholism of the self and the overcoming of the self's fragmentation, but rather the wholism of an ecology of relationships. This larger view of the ecology of relationships to be integrated includes the expectation that the soul is not fully self-dependent in its pilgrimage toward wholeness. By means of God's incarnation in the world and the activity of the Spirit, God is actively engaged in bringing about those changes that makes wholeness ultimately possible.

Integration and wholeness, if seen as goals for change within the theological image of life as pilgrimage, are not, of course, static goals. Rather they point to an open-ended process of movement and change within the structure of life in time. Self-integration thus always participates in the "not-yetness" of the integration of all things in the promise of the coming Kingdom. Wholeness may be found only within the paradoxical tension of the self's life in its history and its eschatologically whole life in the life of God. Thus, when seen theologically, wholeness and integration as goals for pastoral counseling retain a certain ambiguous, even fragmentary quality. The wholeness remains proleptic, a fragmentary anticipation of that final wholeness for which we hope. The pastoral counselor may not, therefore, hope for a "cure" or arrival at some final state of integrated wholeness in the persons with whom pastoral work is undertaken. Rather the looked for outcome is better understood as a removal of certain blockages to integration and an opening of the way toward greater wholeness. Within our hermeneutical theory the blockages most amenable to the work of pastoral counseling will be seen as involving the self's interpretive process—the connections made between meaning and events, relational behavior and the meaning of relationships in the life of the soul.

It may be useful at this point to reflect further on the case of Susan Clark, discussed in the previous chapter, with the view toward developing a more detailed analysis of the goals and limits of change for a pastoral counseling relationship. Even though we have before us only the disclosures she brought into the beginning conversations of counseling, we already are able to see possible directions that therapeutic change might entail.

If we view the disclosed data of Susan Clark's life story with the need for wholeness in mind, we are immediately struck with the diverse themes of her story that appear to lack integration, or, rather, to be held together at an enormous price of pain and dissatisfaction for Susan as well as for members of her family. The dominant theme in the plot of the story of her past adult life seems to be that of duty and obligation. Not only has she faithfully and dutifully worked long hours at two jobs in addition to doing the work of her household, but she experiences her closest relationships to husband, children, and parents within an interpretive metaphor of duty and responsibility. The positive side of her characterizations of self, mother, and husband have been integrated into this story theme of duty and obligation. She sees both mother and husband as good and dutiful people who expect the same of her. But her needs for freedom, autonomy, affection, and excitement in her life have never been integrated into that dominant story theme. Rather these needs are split off from the story of her present life situation and, largely covertly, integrated into the old and deep counter theme of the dislocated adopted child. To this she has given the meaning of unfreedom, painful and undesirable dominance by her adoptive mother, and unexciting, repugnant marriage to a husband who is somehow like mother.

From an object relations perspective it is apparent that this split in the central narrative themes of Susan's self story embodies concomitant splits in her self and object images. Not only is her "good" self (the untiringly dutiful, faithful mother/wife) split from her "bad" self (free, independent, and spontaneously sexual), but also her "good" self is fused to her image of her "good" (dutiful, helpful) mother and her "bad" self is fused with her "bad" mother image (willful, destructive, and dominating). If Susan is to achieve wholeness in her life, these self and object image splits, along with the splits in the deep narrative of her life, must achieve a greater degree of integration. The disintegration she now is experiencing is exacting a terrible price in anger, guilt, anxiety, and a deep sense of empty meaninglessness in her life, together with preoccupation with wishful fantasies of another life she is being denied.

I have already spoken in chapter 6 of the manner in which these splits in the life of Susan's soul have already complicated and impeded her appropriation of the Christian story of a God who is loving and forgiving in the support of human struggles for freedom and reponsible autonomy. For Susan in her present state it would seem that her image of God participates in the same splits that exist in her self and human object images. The God whose wrath she fears and expects if she wrongfully pursues the avenues of her fantasied freedom is split in her mind from the God who will be faithful to her. That God is only available to her if she submits to the life of duty and drudgery she would escape. A new integration of her images of God and her relationship to him can only be achieved as it participates in the reintegration of the total narrative interpretation of her life. As a matter of fact, such a total reintegration may begin at any one of a number of force/meaning nexus points with feedback and further development of the hermeneutical circle providing the avenues for exploration of ramifications of new integrations.

As I reflect on the emotionally and spiritually expensive tenuous integration that Susan Clark's life story up to this time embodies, it is interesting, even mystifying to note how events that occur in apparently random ways shift the balance of narrative integration in the lives of persons. The chance telephone call from an old teen-age romantic partner intruded in Susan's life just at a point at which several things were occurring that were making her life more difficult within the interpretive structure that she had set for herself. Her daughter's arrival at her teen-age years had brought a new note of rebellion and desire for autonomy into her life. That same shift in her daughter's behavior had served to enhance Susan's dependence on her mother for help. The daughter needed more careful supervision, and the grandmother's response had been quite naturally authoritative. Her husband's job change and subsequent difficulties in adjusting to a different set of job expectations had brought to the fore Susan's conflict concerning her images of his capacities. The call from her long lost friend tipped the balance of relative dominance of narrative and object relations themes in favor of the hitherto largely suppressed themes of dislocation and fantasied wish for freedom. The tenuous integration of her life was disrupted. The future plot of her life story took a drastic new turn, at least as wishful possibility. Yet the old dominant themes still held her. A new integration must be undertaken.

Based on the analysis of the self and object image splits we have before us, it would seem that a crucial aspect of any new and creative integration for Susan must include what might well be termed the demythologizing of the old self and object images that now dominate her life narrative. The self and object interpretations that form the characterizations of herself, her mother and husband, perhaps even of her less ambivalently imaged father, need to be reexamined. Do these characterizations actually fit the realities of who these persons are in her present life situation, or are they rather old templates formed in past experience and now being forcefully applied to present relationships? Do the roles she has given herself and others still fit in the present situation?

Here, of course, the pastor who has been privileged to have his or her own opportunity to relate to significant figures in the troubled person's life has a certain advantage, but an advantage accompanied by some prejudicial risk. To have known a family over a period of time in a pastoral relationship set in an ongoing community of relationships such as a parish does provide the pastor with a reality check on the characterizations brought to counseling by a parishioner. Do the images of self and significant other fit the pastor's perception of these persons in their other relationships, including their relationship to the pastor? The risk here is, of course, that such impressions involve the pastor's own interpretations and are therefore subject to the object relational templates he or she brings to human interaction. In some cases the temptation to identify with the characterizations given by the troubled person may be very great indeed. I can, for example, see how a pastor of Susan Clark's home church who had encountered Susan's mother in a difference of opinion over a sermon preached or a decision made in the church could well find a temptation to identify with Susan's characterization of her difficult to refuse!

Many of the human relationship problems that are brought to the pastor's attention, particularly those between the generations, may be understood in terms of the way in which these mythic images of significant others tend to persist through time while at least the conscious self-characterizations have changed. Sons or daughters now in their thirties or forties who complain that a parent has refused to let them grow up may be relating to a dated mythological parent. The reverse may also be true, of course. The parent may be still relating to the mythic image of the son or daughter as a dependent or rebellious child long after the offspring has grown into maturity. The case of Susan Clark demonstrates that these mythological self and object characterizations are most often highly complex, involving image splits of various kinds.

Needless to say, these mythological images, simply because they have deep historical experiential roots, cannot be altered easily or quickly. Simply pointing them out or explaining them is seldom helpful. They tend to permeate all areas of present relationships, even those that to the disinterested observer would have little connection to the relationships with the primary objects. In subtle and highly nuanced ways these core object images can be transferred to important figures in current relationships—husbands (as in Susan Clark's case), wives, co-workers, job supervisors, even pastors.

From the perspective of a hermeneutical theory the process of demythologizing self and object characterizations is a significant aspect of the process described in the previous chapter as the work of the hermeneutical circle. With each movement around the circle from present relationships to historic relationships to the relationship with the counselor, the exploration one by one of the ramifications of narrative and object image themes can open another facet of mythological meaning for reconsideration. With some persons the changes that occur in this process are only slight, the persistence of self and object myths stubborn and unyielding. For others, however, the demythologizing can be profound and the movement toward more realistic imaging of self and others significant enough to support a new direction in the life story.

Puzzling over the problem as to why some are better able than others to carry through what I am calling the demythologizing of self and object images, I find myself making a connection with another facet of hermeneutical theory and applying it to my own clinical experience with the problem. In hermeneutical theory relative to the interpretation of historic texts, the concept is developed that any text contains the possibility of meaning beyond that comprehended by the text's author and intended in the text at the time of its creation. Every text, be that a biblical text or the text of some other historic document, thus may be seen to have a surplus of meaning.[3] Though the author may have intended a particular facet of meaning, the text in itself may be far richer. Other meanings only await actualization in the thought of a reader of the text. Pastors who preach sermons on biblical texts relating them to the contemporary situation quite obviously make use of the surplus of meaning of the text regularly in their interpretations.

In the course of my clinical work with persons who, with my help, were seeking to demythologize their self and object images, I have from time to time encountered an interpretive sequence very much like what hermeneutical theory terms surplus of meaning. A chance memory of an event, an association to a dream, or some other reminder of a past relationship will turn up a facet of that relationship that seemingly has never been appropriated by the person—a facet that has failed to be included in the characterization. If lifted up as significant by either counselor or counselee, such a newly found and memory validated meaning may demand inclusion in the newly forming reconsidered characterization being created in the counseling process.

Warren Biggers, a rather stormy but deeply sensitive man in his forties, had struggled all his life with deep rage and disappointment toward his father. His penchant for angry outbursts at anyone with whom he had conflict was notorious among his acquaintances and often caused him difficulties with both authorities and members of his immediate family. Our explorations in his history indicated that his childhood temper tantrums had often brought him negative attention as a poor substitute for the supportive love that was largely absent in his home in a low income housing unit of a Northern city. Warren was the oldest of a large family of children and, as the oldest, was often the victim of his father's abusive violence when things did not go well in the home. The father, an alcoholic industrial worker, was often drunk in the home and Warren as he grew up became both the spokesman for the family against the father's violent rage and the prime target of the family's complaints.

Warren's deep mythic characterization of his father, and of himself as his father's son, focused heavily on these memories of childhood violence. He saw himself as the angry, stormy, distrustful victim of his father's violent rage.

One day during a counseling session near Thanksgiving, Warren shared a memory of a Thanksgiving of his childhood. It seemed the father had numerous relatives, all of them marginally near the poverty line, many factory workers like his father. This particular holiday the father had invited his relatives for a Thanksgiving feast and had blown most of a pay check on a turkey and all the trimmings. The feast was prepared and was about to begin. But somehow in the conviviality before the meal, an argument was triggered between Warren's father and one of the relatives. The argument escalated into a family row in the course of which Warren's father, already quite drunk, grabbed the table cloth and yanked it hard enough to spill turkey and trimmings in a mess on the floor. The festivities had turned into a fight and the long awaited food virtually turned to garbage.

As Warren and I pondered this painful memory, with Warren emphasizing his bitter disappointment and the verification the memory offered to his mythical characterization of his father as a violent, unloving man, I, quite spontaneously and without great forethought, asked, "I wonder why he invited them?" In the meditative play between us that resulted from my question, the possibility emerged that Warren's father, like Warren, must have had some deep needs for affection, a deep desire for fellowship and closeness with his family. He simply had not been able to bring it off. Too many other forces in his life—his alcoholism, his unhappy marriage, his financial insecurity, and so forth—had interfered.

Another facet of Warren's father's personhood had found its way into our hermeneutical circle. There was more to him than Warren had included in his mythical characterization. In the surplus of meaning of his life history, Warren and I had stumbled onto a new possibility.

Self and object interpretations are always selective. Certain experiences are given symbolic significance and other experiences overlooked. Dominant themes develop that, while most often accurately symbolizing important aspects of relational reality, may obscure other aspects of potentially equal importance. Thus a self or object image may take form that itself represents only a fragment of the whole of a life. Hermeneutical play such as that in which Warren Biggers and I engaged can at times enable persons to alter their mythic images of self and other simply by the inclusion of aspects of old or more recent relationships previously not given significance.

The notion of hermeneutical play in counseling deserves closer examination. Readers will recall that our first encounter with the idea came to us as a key aspect of Hans-Georg Gadamer's concept of the fusion of horizons of understanding. Gadamer proposes that the truly new understanding for both partners in a dialogue (and for both interpreter and a text) emerges when the horizons each partner brings to the interchange have so merged that the dialogue shifts into another level of interaction best understood as a kind of play. My question concerning why Warren's father had invited his relatives to dinner was such a playful question. I did not at the time have anything particular in mind. Yet the question opened up a playful, speculative space between Warren and myself in which both imagination and a more careful attention to the full reality of the remembered situation of the Thanksgiving could interplay. It caused us to imaginatively reconstruct the scene with a fresh, as yet unanticipated possibility providing a new interpretive key.

I am reminded here of D. W. Winnicott's concept of transitional space—that space between the real and fantasy within which the forming self can at once exercise its narcissistic need to control meaning and acknowledge the hard facticity of external reality. Hermeneutical play such as that in which Warren Biggers and I were engaged may be seen as providing a kind of transitional space within which new imaginative interpretations may take form that acknowledge and conform to a larger and richer perception of the reality of a situation than either counselor or counselee had before possessed. The work/play of the counseling hermeneutical circle may thus be seen as being undertaken in the hope and expectation of opening up transitional space within which new and potentially transforming truths, part imaginative interpretation and part new acknowledgment of reality, may come forcefully into play.

Within a theological perspective I would see this hermeneutical transitional space as one of the primary arenas in which the activity of the Spirit may be expected to be found. Stated more modestly and in human terms, it is perhaps rather that it is in the interplay of transitional space that counselee and counselor may become more open to the leading guidance of the Spirit. The Spirit is always active in the gap between humanly constructed reality and the new reality God is bringing about. The hermeneutical play of transitional space may by the grace of God open the participants in that play to such a new reality.

Here we encounter again the ambiguity and paradox that the theological understanding of the process and limits of human change contains. The paradox of historically embedded identity and eschatological identity sets both a hope or expectation and a limit on the quality and degree of change that may be anticipated from pastoral counseling. Theologically speaking, the changes resulting from pastoral counseling will continue to participate in both the "already" and the "not yet" of the fulfillment of the integrative wholeness of the kingdom of God. One side of human paradoxical identity will continue to be in some degree embedded in the history of the person. All that can be hoped for is that the grip of interpretive structuring of historical existence, the historic characterization images and narrative themes, may be loosened enough to make possible a new horizon of self and world understanding. That understanding may in a proleptic fashion embrace more fully the self's eschatological identity.

The case of Susan Clark illustrates the complexity and difficulty of the problem to which a theological perspective points. For Susan the reasons for the selection of fragmentary dominant themes in historical self and object characterizations lie deep in the history of the formation of her self. If my understanding of Susan is at all accurate, it seems clear that, in the interpretive process that has formed her images of herself, her mother, and her husband, she has highlighted only certain meanings that relate to her earliest interpretive dilemma. As an infant she experienced discontinuity in the mothering relationship due to her adoption. I have already discussed the indications that she failed to integrate self and mothering object images at a very early age. The fragmentation of her infancy persists in the shaky foundation of her present mode of imaging her life and relationships. Characterization images whose roots are embedded this deep in personal history may be expected to be particularly difficult to change. Integration of self and object splits, and the inclusion of a wider range of relational memories and possibilities may be expected to be an extended and difficult process. The deep issues in the life of Susan's soul may, within the theological understanding of paradoxical identity, be expected to remain in a fundamental sense unchanged, though the specific shape and dominating force of those issues may be altered to the degree in which, through counseling, she is enabled to grasp her eschatological identity. That grasp must of necessity involve her in acts of creative freedom and response, not only to the counseling relationship, but to the transforming call of God in all the relationships of her life.

A theological perspective thus offers us both a normative direction for evaluating changes taking place in the lives of persons as a result of pastoral counseling and a normative check on our own and our counselees' desires concerning change. Theologically speaking, only those changes that in some way preserve a continuing acknowledgment of individual and corporate human historical embeddedness and the ultimate dependency of the self upon the hope for an ecology of transformed relationships in the transformation of all things will be considered either possible or normatively desirable. Such a theological perspective will stand in sharp contrast to those psychotherapeutic norms for change based upon images of autonomy and individual self-actualization. Such images of human potential for individual growth and self-enclosed freedom will, from this theological perspective, be seen as fundamentally idolatrous and in the end alienating. "We know that the whole creation has been groaning in travail together until now; and not only the creation, but we ourselves, who have the first fruits of the Spirit, groan inwardly as we wait for adoption as sons, the redemption of our bodies. For in this hope we were saved" (Romans 8:22-24 RSV).

Paul here states vividly both the limit and the hope for human change. Change in the final sense for the individual is wrapped up in the hope for change in the whole of creation. Individual human identity is embedded in the great ecology of all things, all relationships. The groaning of individual need for change is but a part of the groaning travail of all creation. The final solution to our desire for creative change must await our adoption as children of God, the redemption of our bodies. The changes we make this side of the not yetness of God's final redemption of creation will all be but fragmentary, proleptic glimpses of that final redemption for which we and all creation hope.

But, says, Paul, we have the first fruits of the Spirit. In that gap between the already and the not yet of eschatological time we may by the power of the Spirit experience changes that bring our historical identity into more wholistic balance with our eschatological identity. Normatively that means that the changes for which we hope and work in our pastoral counseling will be those changes that relate the self more fully and transformatively to all creation, both human relationships and relationships to physical and material things.

The Pauline scripture reminds us also that the work of creative transformation involves both suffering and waiting for the work of the Spirit. Doing the work of suffering is as much a part of a wholistic understanding of opening the way for change in a pastoral counseling relationship as is the play of the fusion of interacting horizons of understanding. Both the helper and the one seeking help must suffer the agonies of change as they await the fruits of change. For the counselee this means suffering at many different levels of intensity and meaning.

There is first the suffering of exposure of those most private and often previously hidden aspects of the life of the soul. As we say it all too easily, the soul must be laid bare, without the benefit of the usual means of protection from self or the counselor. To be most efficacious, that baring of the soul needs to be gradual and carried out at the soul's own pace. At its deeper levels it cannot be forced or carried through on the demand of either counselee or counselor. If rushed or blurted out at too rapid a pace, the process of baring the soul can be aborted as anxiety over a too rapid invasion of privacy becomes overwhelming, demanding defensiveness. Avoidance, denial, or even panic withdrawal from the counseling relationship can be the result of too hasty efforts to lay the soul bare in premature exposure.

For the counselee there is also the suffering of finding that the expectations of the counselor rooted in old narrative themes of the life story do not bring the desired result. Much has been made in the psychoanalytic tradition of the phenomenon of transference in the therapeutic relationship.[4] Within the hermeneutical theory I would see the suffering of the counselee in the transference largely in terms of the painful coming to the realization that old characterization images and narrative theme templates are pervasively involved in present relationships, including that with the counselor. Expectations and demands, wishes and fears concerning response to the issues in the life of the soul are, given time and patient attention by the counselor, brought gradually into the counseling relationship, there to be exposed and interpreted. The result is, of course, a growing and suffering awareness of the help seeker's historical embeddedness. To the degree that the counseling process within the hermeneutical circles it moves in is successful, the counselee will be confronted with a dawning realization that the narrative themes that carry the weight of a historically embedded life cannot be simply discarded, even when insight into history and present interpretive distortions causes the person to want to create an entirely new story for his or her life. For most persons that is suffering of the most frustratingly painful order. So, if counseling is to succeed in its purpose, the help seeker must come to painful grips with the existential limits on the desire to change. An utterly new self with a different history cannot be created. Rather, the narrative of the life of a soul may, with patient, suffering work on the part of both counselee and counselor, undergo degrees of transformative change so that the story of a life may take a new and creative turn.

As there is inevitable suffering for the counselee in the course of a counseling relationship, so also is suffering an unavoidable aspect of the experience of the counselor, if pastoral counseling is to succeed in its purpose. Good counseling, at least good counseling in the hermeneutical mode, cannot be done as an objective, "hands off" exercise of simply instrumental application of learned techniques. To enter with another into hermeneutical examination of the deep issues of that other's soul requires a level of personal involvement and interpersonal engagement that taps the deepest vulnerabilities of the soul of the counselor at a number of different but related levels.

Mention has already been made of the suffering of anxiety that is a necessary ingredient of the counselor's experience when entering newly into a counseling relationship. The beginning stages of any counseling relationship are always fraught with a greater or lesser degree of ambiguity. The counselor quite literally does not know what he or she is getting into. The anxiety of accepting the responsibility for another's welfare without full knowledge of the ramifications of that responsibility can be painful, even when counselors may consciously remind themselves that there are realistic limits on the degree of responsibility one can rightly take for another person. What if the other person becomes suicidal or completely disorganized? Pastors, of course, need to make a realistic assessment of the limits of protection and care that can be provided or be made available to the other person, but even with such boundaries and resources fully known, there still is the painful sense of entering into an unknown situation without benefit of a map or knowing what will be encountered.

This brings us to the second level of suffering on the part of the pastoral counselor having to do with the potential correspondence between the deep issues in the soul of the other person and the issues in the life of the counselor's soul. Narrative themes and characterization images, prevailing emotional valence tones and self and ego conflicts that emerge in the counselee's life story will almost inevitably cut across related issues and themes in the life story of the counselor at both conscious and unconscious levels of awareness. Old issues the counselor thought had been long since put to rest will arise in unexpected ways that require painful self-analysis and reworking. The counselor's self-awareness is repeatedly made vulnerable by the unpredictable ebb and flow of the counseling process and relationship.[5]

A third level of willingness to risk suffering is required of the pastoral counselor with regard to the necessity that the counselor maintain an appropriate balance between objectivity and subjectivity in the counseling process. Without the counselor's ability to enter subjectively into the language and feeling world of the other person, the fusion of horizons of understanding in the transitional space the counseling relationship seeks to create cannot take place. But the counselor's entry into that playful, suffering space must be measured, controlled entry, or the focus of the counseling relationship will be lost. A certain capacity for distanciation—the more objective reflection upon the interaction the counseling engenders—must be maintained. A dialectical tension between engrossment in the process of the counseling and perspective on the process is thus a delicately balanced necessity. The maintaining of that balance often becomes painful to the counselor in that it is experienced as a two-edged sword or a dilemma fraught with considerable risk of error and the necessity to remain self-critical while relating with spontaneity.

Perhaps the most painful levels of suffering made necessary by the counseling role, however, are found in the fundamentally vicarious nature of the counselor's function. I have already discussed the way in which the replaying of old narrative themes and the imposition of old object characterization images lie at the heart of the counseling process. The more significant the counselor becomes to the other person, the more these old relational templates are in multiform fashion thrust wittingly and unwittingly into the counseling relationship by the one seeking help on his or her own terms. Vicariously the counselor becomes the substitute for mother, father, spouse, sibling, or other significant figure in the person's history of relationships. Futhermore, the counselor is thrust into the role of the idealized other by the counselee. The issues of demythologization must be engaged directly in the counseling relationship. To thus be thrust into the mythical role of another is to be subject to both accusation and demanding expectation, both seductive invitation to fulfill old frustrated wishes and blame for inability or unwillingness to gratify fantasied desire. In the midst of that contest between desire and limit, the playing of old story themes and the struggle to find new relational imagery, the counselor must see that the deep issues of the soul are steadfastly confronted. In that situation the counselor suffers both as vicarious target and as the one who with patient authority must see that the issues are faced.

It is at this point in our reflection on the suffering of the counselor that the traditional image of the pastoral relationship as analogous to the incarnation in Jesus can become formative in crucial ways.[6] At the center of the christological image of incarnation is a theology of the cross. Within the Christian story of the cross, the image of vicarious suffering is lifted to an ultimate dimension. In a limited human sense, the vicarious suffering of the pastor embodies the suffering of Christ on behalf of as well as in the place of another. Theologically speaking, the pastor is therefore not left entirely on his or her own in the position of vicarious suffering for the welfare of the other person. The counselor's identity as a follower of Christ, insofar as that identity is taken into the counseling role, provides both a model and an authorization for the suffering work of counseling ministry.

When placed alongside my earlier reflections on the elements of play and transitional, creative space in counseling process, these reflections suggest a full and richly human genre for the story of a pastoral counseling relationship undertaken in the hermeneutical mode. Hermeneutical pastoral counseling is thus not seen as consisting primarily in the application of a learned technique to the solution of individual problems, though certain techniques of listening, reflecting, interpreting, and attending to relational transferences are involved. Beyond or beneath the level of applied techniques, however, the counseling undertaken in this mode is seen to be both wholistically human (play and suffering) and subject to the possibilities and limits of human life in God (the work of the Spirit in the "not yet" of the Kingdom). Empowered by the Spiritual Presence, changes that transform life may take place in and through a counseling relationship. Proleptically, those changes may participate in the in-breaking of the new life of the Kingdom. But, as with all life in the "not yet" of the Kingdom, changed life resulting from pastoral counseling remains paradoxically embedded in history. It is in the hope for both continuing creative change and that final change in the ecology of all things that both counselor and counselee are saved. "But . . . we . . . have the first fruits of the Spirit."

Changing the Story: Myth and Parable in Pastoral Counseling

From chapter 2 onward we have kept at the center of our understanding of change in pastoral counseling Hans-Georg Gadamer's paradigmatic image of the fusion of horizons of understanding. That image complements Boisen's image of the living human document and opens it to the intersubjective dialogue that makes possible altered meanings and, concomitantly, altered life process.

I wish now to press further the methodological application of the image of the fusion of horizons of understanding in pastoral counseling. To do that we will turn to some additional hermeneutical theory concerning the structure of language in stories.

In his book *The Dark Interval: Towards a Theology of Story,* biblical scholar John Dominic Crossan proposes a schema of five ways of using language in the construction of a "world" that story creates and defines.[1] The five ways Crossan suggests are myth, apologue, action, satire, and parable. He schematizes them as follows:

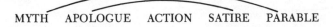

MYTH   APOLOGUE   ACTION   SATIRE   PARABLE

This basic fivefold typology can be summarized like this. Myth establishes world. Apologue defends world. Action investigates world. Satire attacks world. Parable subverts world. It is clear, I hope, that parable can only subvert the world created in and by myth. There is no other world it can touch. It is possible to live in myth and without parable. But it is not possible to live in parable alone. To live in parable means to dwell in the tension of myth *and* parable. It is obvious, of course, that one can change from one myth (for example, capitalism) to another (for example, communism) and that every myth can have an antimyth. But a parable is not an antimyth, and it must be carefully distinguished from such. It is a story deliberately calculated to show the limitations of myth, to shatter world so that its relativity becomes apparent. It does not, *as parable*, replace one myth with another.[2]

Making use in a very softly focused, imagistic fashion of Crossan's typology of the ways of language usage in story, I propose now to analyze the ways of language and relationship usage in pastoral counseling.

Myth

Story - could be true

I have already established that the pastoral counselor, from very early in the counseling relationship, focuses on evoking the underlying mythic narrative of the help seeker's life. It is that mythic story that has constructed the "world" within which the troubled person is seeking to live his or her life. The deep issues of the person's soul are embedded in that world. The pastoral counselor, by evoking the mythic story of the self, seeks to enter the world the story has constructed in order to seek to change it *from the inside*.[3] Following the lead of Anton Boisen, my understanding of the centrality of mythic construction of a world by the person seeking help demands that I take that mythic narrative with great respect and seriousness. In my counseling I will seek so to immerse myself in that world that, insofar as possible, I, too, experience it as from the inside.

Apologue

defense or proof of God

If the language of myth constructs a storied world, apologue defends that world, carries it out in all its ramifications, its nuanced application to every aspect of life in that world. Here comes into view much of particularly the earlier aspects of the pastoral counseling process. As the work of the hermeneutical circle proceeds, both counselor and counselee become more fully aware of the wide and variegated range of relationships, attitudes, feelings, evaluations of self and other behavior, and so on, that the particularity of this way of seeing the world and the self in it entails. The depth and range of this exploration of the ramifications of the self's mythic world will, of course, vary tremendously, depending upon both the length and purpose of the counseling.

For the counselor this means the affirmation and acknowledgment of the possible approriateness, even perhaps the necessity, of the particular mode of mythic construction *at the time in which the interpretation of world was first made*. For the counselee this may mean confrontation with the ways in which that way of envisioning self and world brings difficulty in present reality and present relationships. All that has been said earlier concerning confrontation with historical embeddedness is applicable here. The thrust, however, of the way of apologue is that counselees must be allowed to test fully the limits of the mythical world within which they have sought to live their lives.

The case of Warren Biggers, excerpts of which were discussed in the last chapter, provides a good example of the way in which the language or way of apologue plays an important role in the story of a pastoral counseling relationship. Because of his deep struggle with his father's violent rage and his own identification of himself as like his father in his characterization images, Warren had for years defended his tendency toward temper outbursts as the only "solution" available to him in situations of interpersonal conflict. Such expressions as "I finally had to let her have it!" and "I really nailed him on that!" or "I just had to get my feelings out!" were common in his everyday descriptions of situations outside the counseling hour. Previous counseling with another pastoral counselor had focused largely on his long history of rage and its sources in the relationship to the father. The earlier counseling relationship had been broken off because Warren became enraged at his counselor and was unable to find a way through his anger other than withdrawal from the relationship.

Some weeks into the new counseling relationship with me Warren began to explore very tentatively the limits of his characterization of himself as the angry one who, given his childhood history, had no viable alternative. This exploration took essentially three forms. Historically, he began to explore the deep-lying feelings of abandonment and helplessness that began, with my help, to be imaged as sequentially anterior to the rage and temper outbursts. He began to ruminate about what he must have wanted and needed from his parents that, in his reconstructed story of his life, he never really received. In terms of current relationships Warren began to agonize over the incidents in his life in which his anger, rather than solving problems or bringing him what he desired, only complicated his situation and alienated him from persons with whom he desired and needed relationship. In the counseling relationship with me, Warren began to speak of a taboo we were imposing on his anger as a way of coping with his felt conflicts with me in our conversations. At first he tended to attempt to place responsibility for the taboo on me, saying I was a gentle man who did not believe in or enjoy a good fight the way he did. Later, however, he began to accept shared responsibility for the recognition of the limits on the old way of relating and the search for alternative ways of behaving and imaging himself.

Thus the language of apologue functions in the pastoral counseling relationship both to "defend" the mythic self story and to explore its limits. During the phases of an extended counseling relationship such as I have described with Warren Biggers, the counselor needs to exercise great patience, and insofar as possible, avoid the temptation to impose what Crossan would call an antimyth—a counterposed interpretation of the life story that "corrects" the narrative hermeneutic at work in the counselee's world. Having said that, however, we must recognize that in the counseling relationship itself there most often is what could be called an implicit antimyth: a relationship that, by its regard for the person, its acceptance and sustained interest, may cut across the grain of the mythic story of the world that the counselee brings.

Action

In the "ways of story" schema of John Dominic Crossan the central mode of language is that of action. Action language "investigates" world created by myth. In everyday speech, of course, including the everyday speech that makes up much of a pastoral counseling relationship, this is the language of description. What is happening, has happened or is about to happen in the action of the relational world? But, because the language of action is investigative language, this way of speaking most often is asking variations of the question, What is really happening? What is going on here or what went on in the past? Action language is the language of empiricism. It investigates the world created by myth, asks questions about it, and poses hypotheses about what is going on or will go on within a certain mythic vision concerning the causes and effects of actions and forces given significance within the mythically constructed world.

Here at the most concrete level we encounter the problem of a pluralism of language worlds, a pluralism of mythic images of what the world is and what does or should govern actions in the world. For pastoral counseling this involves all the problems in that regard alluded to in the introductory chapters of this book. As was said there, the pastoral counselor must live on the boundary of a complex pluralism of language worlds seeking to fulfill the role of interpreter and guide.[4] Observation and investigation of the language of actions in human stories always involve some core imagery of the meaning of human action and of the forces that interplay in the causation of behavior. Counselors need therefore to pay close attention to the paradigmatic images that inform their own and their counselees' language of interpretation, implicit or explicit, in their investigative conversations in pursuit of understanding of "what is really going on here."

The language of action in the stories brought to counseling by counselees will ordinarily be variations on the current languages for human behavior and relationships in the popular culture in which the counselee happens to be embedded. In middle-class America these will most often be the popularly psychologized imageries of interpersonal relationships, internal conflicts, self-fulfillment, life stages, and the like. In some persons in the Christian community, particularly in rural or lower-middle-class urban areas, however, the action language may continue to reflect the images of respectability, piety, and moralistically correct behavior of earlier periods of twentieth-century or even nineteenth-century American popular culture. The imagery for describing human action of black or other ethnic community life will be reflected in the languages these persons bring to the task of relating what is going on in their lives.

Whatever the language forms of the counselee, the response of the pastoral counselor will need to be, at least in the beginning, adapted to the imagistic language world of the persons to whom the counselor is relating. Without overtly judging, pro or con, concerning the communicative efficiency or the investigative productivity of the counselee's language of reporting action, the pastoral counselor needs first to hear what the other person has to say on his or her own terms. Images, symbolic words, and key affect-laden phrases can be selected out by the counselor in his or her listening, lifted up as significant, and further investigation invited.

Pastoral counselors will often experience the strong desire to, as it were, teach the counselee a new language for use in day-to-day ordinary speech about human actions and relationships. This is, of course, the attraction of such currently popular language schemas concerning human relationships as transactional analysis (parent, adult, child, scripts, and so forth) and family systems theory (fence, target, control, generational boundary, and the like). The basic problem with aggressive imposition of such approaches from the hermeneutical perspective, helpful as they may be in certain situations, is that in their aggressive application they fail to take with due seriousness the living human document of the counselee(s). A new myth concerning the nature of self and world is superimposed upon the historic one brought by the counselee. Meanwhile the old myth continues to function, though now pushed into the background in the counseling relationship. A contest between myth and antimyth is engendered in which there is considerable risk that the integrative process discussed in the last chaper is not truly fostered.

An example of the problem may serve to elucidate an alternative approach to the problem. Like most pastors who have engaged in marital counseling, I have found myself often sitting with a couple who have encountered difficulty in their marriage and who now engage in long arguments in which each is attempting to blame the other for the problem and convince the other person that the problem could be solved if the other would only change his or her behavior. The language of individual responsibility for evil, blame, accusation, and guilt is still very much alive in American marriages, despite all the efforts of marital self-help manuals, popular psychology books, and articles in every "family" magazine from *Readers Digest* to *Psychology Today* to introduce a new language for marital interaction. "Who's at fault" continues to be a favorite way of marital partner investigation!

The Christian pastor who hears this kind of accusatory marital interaction will most certainly long, as I have, for the power to shift the language of inquiry concerning the problem in a more wholeheartedly Christian direction. For the language of blame, accusation, guilt, and shame we would substitute a language couched more in the images of forgiveness, acceptance, repentance for past failings, and recognition of mutual responsibility to love. My experience is, however, that efforts to impose that language on couples locked into an accusatory investigative contest will most often be anything but successful. The leap from the way of charge and countercharge to acceptance and deeply felt and expressed forgiveness is simply too great to make by sheer act of will, even when the longing to do so is present, to say nothing of those more difficult cases in which the desire itself seems to have been lost along the way.

If the leap from the language of fault to the language of acceptance is too great to be made directly, what is perhaps needed is a transitional language that begins to undermine the language of fault with a new level of understanding of the differing perceptions of the realities of behavioral actions in the marital process. Two differing horizons of understanding need a vehicle to assist them in the process of merger that the Christian language of acceptance presupposes. Investigation that assists in clarifying marital communication can help in that transition.

Various psychological constructions of marital dynamics offer ways of imaging differences between marriage partners and the manner in which marital communication can become skewed or blocked that can begin to reshape the interactive investigation of what really went or goes on between partners devoid of blame, fault, and accusation. Used in this way as transitional languages, psychological language images may help open the way toward shifting the emotional and descriptive content of conversation about marriage problems more in the direction of a language of acceptance.

Pastors who envision their work with marriage partners in conflict within the framework of a hermeneutical theory will, however, take care to avoid introduction of these psychological language schemas as a new technology for marriage relationships. Their secondary place as transitional languages needs to be maintained. It is, in fact, more important that the pastor utilize the conceptualizations that the psychological approaches to marital dynamics present to enrich and inform the usage made of more ordinary words familiar to the persons with whom the pastor is working, rather than to introduce a new set of psychological terms as the "correct" language. I have found, for example, that some of the current psychological writings dealing with marriage "contracts" can be helpfully utilized to enrich and particularize work with couples in relation to reflection on the more historically religious notion of covenant in marriage. Talk about marriage contracts can provide a good transition to talk about marriage covenants that embraces a language of acceptance and mutual respect.[5]

ridicule in exposing - emphasizes the weakness more than the weak

Satire

The way of satire in any story is the way of seeking to destroy a mythic way of seeing things by lampooning it. Satire holds before us the myths of our lives so that the angle of our vision reveals their absurdity. Satirical stories invite us to laugh at ourselves. Life as we have constructed it is revealed, at least for the moment, as ridiculous. Satire loosens the control of our myths upon us.

Is there a place for satire in pastoral counseling? I believe there is, though, like satirical humor in social interaction generally, it is best when found in small, well-placed doses.

One of the more useful ways of satire is the way of exaggeration. The mythic way by which we have seen things is pushed beyond its limits. Change is invited by means of asking indirectly just how far the other person is willing to press a certain way of imaging the world. If a relationship of trust has been well established in a pastoral counseling relationship, exaggeration can be useful.

Recently a couple with whom I have worked in marriage counseling for some time began to engage, as I had heard them do before, in a heated discussion of a recent disagreement over some relatively minor incident involving their relationship to a member of the husband's family. "Whenever she and I get into something, you always take her side," said the husband. "You never support me in anything where my family is concerned!" "And you always get defensive around your family!" retorted the wife. "You never can stand on your own feet in relation to your sister particularly!"

After this went on for some minutes, I began breaking in whenever I heard the words "always" or "never" by loudly and with as much conviction as I could muster repeating: "ALWAYS!" "NEVER!" My purpose was, of course, both to attack the mythic characterizations of each other being so blatantly evidenced and to force a confrontation with the ridiculous humor of this way of seeing the other person. After the process was repeated several times we all broke into at first anxious and then hilarious laughter. There followed a much quieter reflective conversation about the way in which their expectations of each other tend to become stereotypical and self-serving.

The way of satire in pastoral counseling can also be the way of sarcasm and irony. Retelling a story brought by a counselee or helping the person to reconstruct the story so it sounds a little like a Doonesbury comic strip can, if the timing is right, hold before the other the imagery, characterizations, and tones of the story in such a way as satirically to attack a way of shaping a world and seeing one's place in it. Like exaggeration, sarcasm and irony are best administered in small, carefully timed doses, lest the other person experience the attack on his or her world as rejection or hostility. Change can be seen as humorously, ridiculously, or ironically necessary, but satire administered with too heavy a hand can spell injury and lack of respect.

Parable

conveys meaning indirectly by use of comparison

The way of parable is, says Crossan, the way of subversion. Rather than seeking to change the world that myth has constructed from outside, as in the way of antimyth, or to attack it by ridicule, as in satire, the way of parable involves changing the mythic world from inside by means of subverting it, giving it a new twist so that a fresh possibility is opened.

As is the case with the parables of Jesus, the well-told parable begins with an ordinary event or set of events from everyday life. A story is begun that has a familiar ring. But as the story progresses a radically new and unexpected turn is taken that breaks open the boundaries of expectation in the mind of the hearer of the parable. The set expectations of the mythic construction of world are subverted; something radically new is introduced that, while respecting the world of myth, shatters its limits and expands its horizons.[6]

In her book *Speaking in Parables*, theologian Sallie McFague speaks of parables as "extended metaphors," which is to say that they have the capacity to open up a way of life that extends beyond the brief flash of new insight they may engender.

A parable is an *extended* metaphor—the metaphor is not in discrete images that allow for a flash of insight (a purely aesthetic or intellectual "Aha!"), but it is a way of believing and living that initially seems ordinary, yet it is so dislocated and rent from its usual context that, if the parable "works," the spectators become participants, not because they want to necessarily or simply have "gotten the point" but because they have, for the moment "lost control" or as the new hermeneuts say, "been interpreted." The secure, familiar every-dayness of the story of their own lives has been torn apart; they have seen another story—the story of a mundane life like their own moving by a different "logic," and they begin to understand (not just with their heads) that another way of believing and living—another context or frame for their lives—might be a possibility for *them*.[7]

McFague here suggests several things concerning the event of parabolic insight, all of which are compatible with Crossan's notion of parable as subversion. She suggests that parables are far more than simply stories with a point or lesson to teach. Rather they are those subversive events of experienced insight in which the hearer becomes participant in a new way of seeing an ordinary experience of life in such a way as to, for the moment, lose control or be freshly interpreted by the experience. A new "logic" is introduced that, while respecting and carrying along with it the mythic story of the past, opens up the possibility of a new "context" or "frame" for the person's life. The metaphor implicit in the parabolic experience gains the possibility of being extended.

In my earlier book, *Crisis Experience in Modern Life,* I introduced the notion of parabolic experience as a way of speaking of experiences that may take place outside the pastoral counseling relationship, but which at times may become tranformative parabolic experiences through the process of interpretive reflection in the counseling relationship.[8] I described there several such experiences that took place in the course of my work in counseling with Mrs. Reed, the person with whom I first began to think of pastoral counseling in terms of life experience stories as potentially parabolic experiences.

Subsequent to my work with Mrs. Reed in the early 1960s, I have come to an increasing appreciation of the manner in which fragments of life experience, with proper attention, can become parabolic vignettes breaking open long established ways of seeing self and world. Given such attention on a continuing basis, they may develop into extended metaphors providing a new frame of interpretation continuous with the historically embedded identity yet transformative in their impact.

The best parables in pastoral counseling most often are those that simply happen at the "right time" in the counseling process, rather than those that the counselor may seek to insert as illustrative or suggestive stories. The counselor does not have to tell a story; the parabolic story happens in the counselee's experience and is then appropriated as parable. An experience that occurs spontaneously holds greater power to "interpret" the experiencer than a story told by another. Such experienced parables exhibit the power of being unmistakably one's own, yet also in a curious way are experienced as happening *to* the person from beyond his or her own doing. This duality of perspective may on occasion carry the impact of a revelatory experience disclosing ultimately significant truth.

The following case example illustrates the manner in which parabolic experiences in counseling may become extended metaphors that institute, by their power to interpret the experiencer, a new frame or context for living. The case also illustrates the complex ways in which a duality of perspective (my own experience, yet it happened *to* me) can on occasion engender a whole new frame of reference, a new dimension that qualitatively transcends the person's old way of seeing his or her life.

Tim Lyon, a professional architect in a large metropolitan firm, was referred for pastoral counseling by his pastor because of his periodic bouts of depression, increasing dependence on alcohol, and growing marital crisis due to his drinking and emotional absence from the home. In his forties and the father of two young sons, nine and twelve, Tim had struggled all his life with feelings of inadequacy and inability to perform up to the expectations of either his wife or the senior members of his firm—the latter in spite of the fact that from outward appearances he was respected for his careful, albeit laborious and unspectacular work. Of his marriage he said that all had gone well during the courtship while engaged in his professional training, "then when we were married, life suddenly got very serious!"

Tim had been raised an only child by a mother he described as very anxious and fearful and a father who, though he was at the time of Tim's birth an officer in a small town bank, was soon to become a hopeless and increasingly helpless alcoholic. Some of Tim's most painful childhood memories were of occasions when he and his father would go together to a college football game, Tim with high expectations and his father with a bottle in his pocket. By the end of the game the father would be too drunk to find the car and Tim, still in his preteens, would have to help his father home as best he could, only to find his mother in tears and needing his comfort and support. Feelings of inadequacy for the task coupled with an internalized enormous demand to achieve ran deep in Tim's self-characterization.

Needless to say, the pastoral counseling process with Tim Lyon was long and laborious, fraught with numerous setbacks and much struggle to achieve at first sobriety and then self-acceptance and appropriate esteem. The details of the counseling are both too extensive and unnecessary to share for our limited illustrative purpose. Rather I wish to focus on a single parabolic experience that became an extended metaphor around which Tim began to organize a new and transformed frame of interpretive reference for his life. Readers should keep in mind the relative significance of this experience. It did not in and of itself evoke change. Rather, when appropriated in the context of other experiences both within and outside the counseling, it became highly symbolic as a new organizing center or frame for finding a new direction of meaning for Tim's living.

Tim had for some time been interested in environmental conservation and, without very much psychological reflection, had traded in his old personal car, an American-made gas guzzler, on a stick-shift Volkswagen Rabbit. As I recall it, some slight reference was made at the time of the purchase to the Rabbit's being a car "more my size." Not long after beginning to drive the new Rabbit to work, one day Tim was leaving his office on his way to see me at the end of the day when he encountered in the office parking garage one of his associates in his firm as they both headed for the one-lane exit. The other person, a highly aggressive and success-oriented younger colleague, was driving a new silver Mercedes, complete with sun roof and leather upholstery. As they approached the exit, the colleague, with a wave of the hand and a surge of high-performance power, zipped ahead to claim the first chance to get ahead of the traffic. "I putted on out in my VW and have been thinking all the way out here about whether I belong in the Rabbit or if I want to drive in the fast lane with my buddy in the silver Mercedes."

Tim and I reflected together for the better part of that counseling hour on this vignette that so symbolized his struggle to make peace with his history and his desires for his life. The experience thrust upon him the element of choice with which he was confronted. It not only interpreted for Tim who he was and might be, it somehow contained an element of urgency to get on with it and make some kind of exit from the way he had for a long time downplayed his considerable abilities while fantasizing that he could never meet the external expectations placed upon him.

The incident passed, but in the long months ahead the parabolic quality it contained became an extended metaphor for Tim's struggle to make peace with his life and situation. Other metaphors emerged from the symbol of the car he was to drive. We began to speak of "fast lanes" and "slow lanes." I introduced the notion of a "middle lane." At one point during a time of resurgent ambition, Tim impulsively traded the Rabbit for an expensive and flashy sports convertible. But he was never satisfied with it; it cramped his tall body and made his back ache on long trips.

Meanwhile Tim began to show signs of claiming the skills he had in his work and being less threatened by the expressed wishes of his wife for more participation and spontaneity in the life of the family. Other incidents occurred which pressed him to accept some of his limitations, while yet valuing his abilities. At one point this new frame of interpretation for his life again focused on the purchase of a new car, this one neither Mercedes nor Rabbit, but a highly regarded, respectable, and somewhat expensive Volvo small sedan. "It's a good car for the middle lane, and I just couldn't bring myself to settle for a fifty-mile-to-the-gallon Toyota!"

It is important to recognize that in many respects Tim, following his appropriation of the new extended metaphor the parking garage incident initiated, remained the same person. The question of abilities and demands of life remained a deep issue in his soul. Yet the old mythic frame within which he had struggled with that issue had been subverted: he began to experience a degree of choice in his life that had been missing before.

John Dominic Crossan, in another book, titled *In Parables: the Challenge of the Historical Jesus,* interprets the parables of Jesus in the Gospels within a framework of time in relation to the kingdom of God. For Crossan the parables proclaim the kingdom's temporality and the three simultaneous modes of its presence.[9] These three modes are its *advent* as gift of God, its *reversal* of the recipient's world, and its empowering of life and *action*.[10]

Parables of advent are the parables of joy in discovery. Something heretofore hidden in mystery is revealed in a form unmistakably recognizable. The parables of the lost sheep and the lost coin and the mustard seed are typical of this group of parabolic sayings in the Gospels. In each case the distinguishing characteristic of advent parables is that something extraordinary is found in something very ordinary. The mustard seed grows into a great tree; the lost coin is found to be of extraordinary value worth selling all one has to possess; and so forth.

In pastoral counseling I have frequently encountered parabolic experiences that have about them this advent quality. A small and seemingly insignificant experience is suddenly, even mysteriously, seen to contain a key element of the life the person has longed or vaguely wished to possess. The experience contains an intimation of the possibility of transcendence. In a sense Tim Lyon's discovery, though it would take many months of further work in counseling to flesh out the full ramifications of that choice.

> In a religious metaphor, as we shall see in the parables, the two subjects, ordinary life and the transcendent, are so intertwined that there is no way of separating them out and, in fact, what we learn is not primarily something about God but a new way to live ordinary life.[11]

Here Sallie McFague suggests the possibility that, though the language of God or the kingdom was not involved in Tim Lyon's appropriation of his parabolic experience in the parking garage, at an implicit level, something transcendent was in the process of occurring. Certainly, as Tim worked through the extended metaphor of the experience, he drew closer to claiming his eschatological identity as a child of the Kingdom than he was before while living with the burden of self-expectation that included his inability to perform comfortably on the "fast track." In that sense the parabolic experience came to him as a "gift of God."

The parking garage experience was even more clearly a parabolic experience of reversal. The structure of ambition and failure that had so plagued Tim in his work and marriage was in the sharp and clear picture of the colleague in the silver Mercedes turned against itself. He saw the other person as not only the person he was not, but as the person who, given his history and life situation, he no longer wanted to be. His vision for his life underwent a revision in a more modest direction. That new vision was to be tested again and again in subsequent events in his life, including the abortive effort to ride the fast track in the expensive sports car. But the old way of seeing himself in the mode of failed ambition had begun to be reversed.

Parables of action are, according to Crossan, parables that "portray crucial or critical situations which demand firm and resolute action, prompt and energetic decision."[12] The parables of the friend at midnight, the unjust judge, and the rich fool are examples of parables of Jesus in this mode. Urgency and momentously symbolic choice characterize the experiencing of such parabolic happenings.

The parking garage parabolic experience, particularly if seen in its extended metaphorical context, certainly contained for Tim Lyon the quality of increased urgency of decision. Peace must be made between the two poles of his self-characterization symbolized by the Rabbit and the Mercedes. Either he had utterly to change who he was in order better to conform to the mythic image of the man in the silver car on the fast life track or he must adapt his life-style and expectations in conformity with his more modest and realistic self assessment. In either case the old mythic self-characterization had been subverted.

The questions Tim continued to struggle with during the active period of the metaphor's extension were thus both questions of self-acceptance and of compromise concerning life goals. This involved momentous choice not only in terms of a more genuine valuing of the assets he had and what Erik Erikson would call "repudiation" of the utter necessity of those qualities he did not, by virtue of his reclaimed history, possess: qualities now associated with the "fast lane."[13]

The Pastoral Counselor as Parabolic Figure

In John Dominic Crossan's account of the formation of the early church, an important transition was made in the transformation of the role of the historical Jesus as parabler into the role of Jesus as the Parable of God.

> The parabler becomes parable. Jesus announced the Kingdom of God in parables, but the primitive church announced Jesus as the Christ, the Parable of God. . . .
>
> The Cross replaced the parables and became in their place the Supreme Parable.[14]

This image of the Christ of the cross as the Supreme Parable of God, who in the event of the cross subverted the mythic Jewish narrative of the creator God as King of the Universe, is, of course, an extension of the image at the center of that level of time referred to earlier as eschatological time. The Christ of the cross subverts historical time into the dimensions of the time of God's activity in creation and history. The ordinariness of historical time becomes the extraordinariness of God's disclosure and engagement of created life. Through the Incarnation, God becomes the Subverting Presence in historical existence whereby the transforming power of the Kingdom is made present to us.

Here comes into view a fresh possibility for the analogical appropriation of incarnational theology for the ministry of pastoral care and counseling. As the Christ of the cross was the Supreme Parable of God, so we pastors may seek to become parabolic figures with those who come to us for help with their problems of historical existence. Within the parabolic imagery, our ministry becomes one of subversion, of seeking to change the mythic narratives of others' lives from the inside by the quality of our presence with them. The pastoral relationship itself should then become parabolic, giving to the narrative of the other person a new twist that opens the story to a fresh and lively possibility. Like the good parable, the pastoral relationship may be one of advent or gift, of reversal of the recipient's world, and of empowerment for action. But also in the mode of the good parable, the good pastoral relationship remains in the lower case; in its ordinariness, its human everydayness, it represents and, on occasion, discloses the extraordinary—the gift of God.

The Ending Phase:
Pastoral Counseling and
the Community of the
Christian Story

This chapter has a dual purpose, the two aspects of which are interrelated. Having examined the core problem of change in pastoral counseling from several methodological perspectives, we need now to consider the signs of change on the basis of which a decision to end a formal pastoral counseling relationship may be made. That task cannot, however, be given adequate consideration without reflection on the larger context within which *pastoral* counseling takes place: the context of the Christian community. I shall therefore attempt to develop an understanding of formal counseling's ending phase in the light of that context. The Christian community and its story both support pastoral counseling and provide the context of care to which the continuing life of the soul of the person who has sought counseling is committed.

Here I am reminded again of an important difference between the contextual presuppositions of the pastoral counselor and those of the typical secular psychotherapist. Set within the secular therapeutic tradition of the "treatment" of "disorders" or "illness," secular psychotherapists tend to see the ending phase of psychotherapy as preparation of patients or clients for life "on their own." Ending a psychotherapeutic relationship means terminating the therapeutic context in favor of life in the context of the "real world." A psychotherapeutic case thus begins with the presentation of a human problem in the therapeutic context and ends when the problem has been sufficiently resolved to make possible life without "therapy."

Pastoral counseling undertaken in the hermeneutical mode developed in this book assumes a somewhat different context, the context of human life seen as pilgrimage set within a community that shares a certain narrative vision or mythos concerning the whole of life in creation. The care provided by pastoral counseling is thus only one aspect of a larger context of care provided by the community of faith and life. Rather than "treating" an "illness" or "solving" a "problem," the pastoral counselor seeks to provide a more or less temporary intensification of a process of care and prophetic ministry to persons which the church in its ministry in other modes carries on with people throughout their lives. The deep issues of the soul with which pastoral counseling is primarily concerned are the same issues as those with which ministry is concerned in preaching, worship, Christian education, and pastoral care. What pastoral counseling makes possible is simply an intensification and greater particularization of ministering response to the specificity of those issues. The solving of human problems is seen as fundamentally related to coming to grips with the deeper issues in the life of the soul. Human problems provide the occasion for the surfacing of these deeper issues.

Ministering to persons in relation to the deeper issues in the life of the soul or the personal problems of their lives is not, of course, the only ministry in which the Christian community is engaged. The church also has a mission in the larger community and the world beyond concern for the welfare of its own members. The scope of my interest in this book, however, directs our attention to the Christian community context as a locus for the care of souls within that community.

Given the life cycle and Christian community context for pastoral counseling, four sets of issues come into focus relative to the ending phase of pastoral counseling. First, there is the issue of referral of persons ending an intense phase of counseling back to the ordinariness of life in the community of faith. Second, there is a cluster of issues that center around the question as to the degree of control the counselor can and should exercise with regard to outcomes of the counseling process. Third, and closely related to that set of problems, is the cluster of issues relative to pastoral counseling with persons who have no viable relationship with a community of faith. This latter set of issues might be termed the question of the pastoral counselor's responsibility for evangelism. Finally there are those issues concerned with the relationship of care and service.

The problem of referral in pastoral counseling has usually been considered from the standpoint of assisting persons experiencing problems of living in their search for specialized help.[1] Important as that ministry of referral is, the task of assisting persons ending a counseling relationship is of equal significance. Whether the persons receiving counseling have or have not been members of an active community of faith during the counseling process, the ending phase of intense work on the deeper issues of their lives in a counseling relationship brings to the fore the question as to how the process of self-formation is to be continued and nurtured. Persons ending a counseling relationship are now in need of appropriating a faith community in new ways so that their pilgrimage may continue to find support and creative challenge.

Particular attention to the shift of the primary locus of self-formation from the counseling relationship to the community of faith is needed not only because the pilgrimage of life in the tensions of paradoxical identity is never fully completed within the boundaries of finite human existence, but also because the sustaining of such a pilgrimage is fundamentally a social process. Only a community of shared vision and narrative structure can meaningfully sustain the level of continuing dialogue and shared experience that makes the continuation of a Christian life of pilgrimage possible. Through experiences of shared worship and liturgy, the continuing process of interpretation and reinterpretation of the paradigmatic images and texts of the community's life through preaching and the educational life of the church, and, most of all, through the sustaining power of a shared ethos of faith and meaning, the soul of the pilgrim finds a contextual home for the journey that must be continued after counseling has ended.[2]

It must be recognized, of course, that local Christian churches vary tremendously in both the quality of their corporate life as a community of shared narrative vision and in the level of their hospitality toward persons seeking a context for further growth in relation to the deeper issues of the soul. Ideally the church should be a community in which the deep narrative structure of the Christian life is not only regularly and imaginatively ritualized and celebrated, but also is probed and reinterpreted in ways that stretch the limits of that narrative as a structure of meaning and purpose for living at both personal and societal levels. For the individual Christian this means that the local community of faith should be a source of both support and challenge toward further integration and growth. But, as Jurgen Moltmann reminds us, the identity of the church, like that of the individual, is a paradoxical identity.[3] It is itself a community both embedded in history and called to participate in the incoming of the Kingdom. So the level of a particular local church's capacity to fulfill its purpose vis-à-vis the individual will vary greatly. As a matter of fact, it is not unusual for persons who have engaged in the deep probing of their lives that counseling over a period of time entails, to have difficulty finding a church or a group within a church in which they feel a kinship of common concern. For such persons the typical church activity and fellowship may seem banal and superficial. Pastoral counselors need to give specific attention to both encouraging and supporting persons ending counseling in their search for the best context for their continued life of faith and growth and to exercise the new vision they have received through counseling in sensitizing the church to the needs of others. More about that later.

The second set of issues that comes into focus in relation to the larger community context in which persons ending counseling must continue their pilgrimage has to do with recognition of limits on control of outcome. Pastoral counseling in the hermeneutical mode, though it takes with utter seriousness the role of the counselor as representative of the Judeo-Christian horizon of understanding, does not presuppose that counselees will all therefore appropriate the narrative structure of Christian faith for their living. Implicit in both the paradigmatic image of the self as living human document and the image of change as brought about through a fusion of horizons of understanding is a basic respect for the authority of the individual soul hermeneutically to structure its own life. In the interactive play and suffering of the fusion of horizons, the horizon of Christian understanding is put at risk fully as much as the horizon brought by the help-seeker. The power of its symbols and meanings is tested in the crucible of examination of the struggles of an individual soul with the concrete problems of historical existence. The outcome of that process cannot be, nor should it be, predetermined. A process is set in motion that must be trusted even though its future is subject to human error as well as to the activity of God on behalf of the person. Theologically speaking this means that the pastoral counselor places his or her trust in the workings of the Spirit. Final outcomes are left to a larger process than simply that of counseling itself.

In practice, however, there emerges a significant facet of the issue of outcome having to do with the difference between counseling with a person who has a history of significant involvement in the Christian community or who was reared within that tradition and counseling with the person who has never been exposed to that tradition beyond the exposure of a general culture shaped by secularized Christian history. In the first instance it is reasonable to expect that the outcome of faithfully conducted pastoral counseling in the hermeneutical mode will include alterations in the individual's appropriation of Christian symbols and meanings. Through the impact of both the implicit representation of the Christian horizon in the counseling relationship and, on occasion, the explicit interplay of conversation concerning Christian modes of meaning, the counseling process may be expected to have significant impact. Old historic appropriations of Christian symbols and story may be reconsidered at both conscious and unconscious levels. For these persons the ending phase of counseling can quite naturally and informally include consideration of the question concerning where and with whom the process of Christian reflection on life process is to be continued.

Pastoral counseling with persons whose life narratives prior to counseling have not included significant appropriation of the Christian narrative and its symbols presents a somewhat different set of outcome issues. To what extent can or should pastoral counseling be expected to fulfill an evangelistic function relative to the active solicitation of the counselee's participation in and commitment to a community of Christian faith? Does such an evangelistic purpose run counter to the central purpose of counseling in the hermeneutical mode, namely, the changing of a life narrative "from the inside"? Does not the counselor's openness to the horizon of the other place significant constraints upon the manner in which counseling can be expected to fulfill an evangelistic purpose?

It is perhaps important to acknowledge that reflection on this issue in our time is made more difficult by virtue of the imagistic connotations that the term evangelism has come to carry in particularly American Protestant circles. The images the word tends to generate are of more or less aggressive "witnessing" to others concerning the crucial importance of Christian faith commitment. Few pastoral counselors wish to see their counseling as having that form of evangelical purpose. Yet, in a larger and somewhat softer sense the basic theological structure that undergirds the hermeneutical theory, as I have already indicated, presupposes that the pastoral counselor functions as representative and therefore in some sense as advocate of the Christian mythos. In the quality of his or her presence in the relationship, whether that be as parabolic figure, partner in the play and interplay of fused horizons, or as one who suffers in the ways described in chapter 7—in all these ways the pastoral counselor "witnesses" to the horizon of Christian faith that undergirds his or her presence. In the disciplined freedom of the counseling situation the pastoral counselor's commitment to the Christian vision may and most often will on occasion be made explicit.

One possible result of pastoral counseling in this mode may thus be what amounts to a form of conversion experience. The life narrative that, prior to counseling, had not appropriated the symbols and images of Christian faith may have become so fused with the horizon of the counseling process informed by those images that the personal narrative structure begins to be intertwined with elements of the Christian narrative structure. The extent and degree of open acknowledgment of that new fusion will vary considerably from person to person. But to whatever degree that has occurred, the pastoral counseling will have indeed fulfilled an evangelistic purpose and must accept a share of responsibility for the outcome, for good or ill! With such persons the stance of the pastoral counselor during the ending phase of counseling will involve a delicate blending of respect for the individual's right to pursue his or her pilgrimage in ways that seem appropriate to the person and affirmation of the other's search for a social context in which to make that pursuit. For the parish pastor as counselor this may mean the exercise of a certain dispassionate objectivity concerning a possible difference between what is best for this person and what might be desirable from the perspective of adding new converts for his or her church.

Ambiguity of specific outcome to pastoral counseling means, of course, also ambiguity of moral and spiritual outcome. Pastoral counseling thus participates in the ambiguity of any human enterprise. It does not, nor can it, ensure the moral correctness, or lasting quality of its outcome. This does not, however, excuse the pastoral counselor from the exercise of appropriate concern for the direction that outcome is to take. Christian pastoral counseling does mean concern for outcome more fully participating in the fruits and possibilities of the Kingdom.

A fourth set of issues that pastoral counseling's ending phase brings into focus emerges from what might well be called the parabolic twist that the full appropriation of the Christian gospel entails. From what we have said up to this point concerning the return of the counselee to the ordinariness of life in the Christian community, it may appear that life in that community is primarily made up of receiving nurture and support for the life of the self. But that is clearly not the case; life as a member of the community of faith in the crucified God is life in service and hopeful expectation of the Kingdom. It is life in which the very fact of one's own suffering is turned to creative purpose. Human weakness becomes strength; human poverty of spirit is turned into a valuable asset in opening the self to the suffering of others.

The ending of a phase of specialized and particularized care for the life of the soul should thus be marked by a turning away from primary concern for the self and its welfare toward concern for others. The clarifying awareness of the depths and complexity of the suffering in one's own soul needs to be turned toward the expression of greater sensitivity to the suffering of others.[4] As a matter of fact, an important aspect of the Christian community context for pastoral counseling is its continuing reminder both during and after counseling that the preoccupation of the person with the self and the soul's issues, necessary as it is, is temporary and instrumental to the larger purposes of the Christian life beyond the needs of self. Here the Christian context, if fully appropriated by both counselor and counselee, embodies a peculiar reversal of many of the values of contemporary culture with its penchant toward the centering of life in the fulfillment of the self. Just how that reversal of values is to be expressed both implicitly and explicitly in the counseling relationship, particularly in its ending phase, will vary from case to case. But, if pastoral counseling is to be an expression of the gospel in its fullest sense, the reversal will reveal itself and find some appropriate affirmation.

Signals of the Ending Phase of Counseling

Having considered some of the implications of the contextual presuppositions of pastoral counseling in the hermeneutical mode with regard to the ending phase of counseling, I now turn our attention to the matter of the signals of counseling's ending phase. What are the behavioral, hermeneutical, and relational signs that indicate the arrival of the ending phase? It must be kept in mind, of course, that, like beginning counseling, ending is a relative matter. Some will want to end counseling when a particular felt problem has been worked through to the person's satisfaction. Others will end the process when their level of anxiety or other troublesome feeling has receded sufficiently for the individual to continue his or her pilgrimage without the help of a counselor. Still others will withdraw prematurely when the deeper issues of their souls are only beginning to emerge. I will, however, assume here that there has been sufficient time and effort given to counseling for some of the experiences of the hermeneutical circle described in earlier chapters to take place. What then are the signals of transition back into the everydayness of living and the appropriate ending of the intensity of self-examination that counseling entails?

1. *Signals of integration and wholeness.* These signals are perhaps easier to recognize than they are to write about descriptively. In the clinical context they are often first recognized as signs of a higher level of the sense of well-being than that exhibited earlier in the counseling relationship. Body posture and movement, the appropriateness and spontaneity of affect, and shared evidence of involvement in everyday living all begin to signal a new level of whole-person engagement of life in all its aspects. Signals of higher (for the person) available energy levels speak of a receding of the levels of energy being utilized to hold old conflicts at bay. Blind spots in conversation concerning significant relationships in the person's life are less frequently apparent and troublesome. Mood swings are less violent and, when present, more appropriately related to current events in living. Self-esteem and self-criticism have begun to be both more realistic and less a matter of daily concern.

As the person enters a desirable ending phase, the pastoral counselor who has come to know the mythic world of the individual soul from the inside will be monitoring the manner in which old fragments of self and other characterizations, old threads of life story plots, and old dissociated affective ties have begun to gather themselves around new and transformed ways of seeing and experiencing self in relation to world. Has a certain realism begun to find its way into the life story that embraces both the positive and the negative, a sense of both what has been good and what has been evil, a sense of both possibility and limit in the life of the self?

2. *Signals of altered behavior and altered relationships.* Even though it may appear that the emphasis of a hermeneutical theory may have been placed heavily on the process of changing interpretations of meaning rather than on altering behavioral patterns, one of the important signals of appropriate ending of counseling is indeed altered behavior in relationships. This is true because one of the presuppositions of pastoral counseling in the hermeneutical mode is that behavior and meaning are interlocking forms of human expression. As was earlier proposed by means of extrapolations from Ricoeur's interpretation of Freud's psychoanalytical theory, the dynamics of human behavior are force/meaning dynamics. Behavior expresses meaning just as meaning is the symbolic interpretation of significance of behavior. Altered meaning structures therefore go hand in hand with altered patterns of behavior.

Given these presuppositions of the theory with regard to behavior and meaning, behavioral signals of counseling's ending phase might therefore be expected to be characterized by a certain congruency between behavior in relationships and the emerging transformations in meaning patterns the counseling has evoked. To the degree that behavior in significant relationships is incongruent with emerging patterns of transformed meaning, it may be assumed that the transformative process has remained on a superficial level and has failed to penetrate those levels of interpretation and meaning at which force/meaning dynamics actually function to shape personhood. On the other hand, if behavior toward significant others has changed in ways that conform to newly emergent meanings, then it may be assumed that a deeper level of significant transformation has taken place.

The example of Tim Lyon in chapter 8 is perhaps illustrative of the interlock between changing patterns of interpretation and altered behavior. Tim's purchase of the expensive sports convertible midway in the process referred to as the extended metaphor was behavior that expressed his desire to leap above or outside his history and the meaning it had come to have for him. At that point I recall his expressing the wishful hope that the act of buying and driving the car would "do something" for him. But the incongruity of the sports car and his emerging sense of being an able but limited person was soon made apparent, both behaviorally (he could never feel at home driving the car) and in terms of its meaning ("That's not where I am!"). Only when he began more realistically to accept and value who he was could his behavior in the purchase of a new and different kind of car express who he was becoming more free to be. It is both interesting and important to recognize that the puchase of the relatively expensive sedan expressed the continuing polarity of his self-understanding and the dynamic force conflicts of his life. It was more expensive than a Toyota, but less incongruently flashy than the sports car. It held together his old conflict, but in a new and more realistic way.

3. *Signals of clarity concerning the continuing issues in the life of the soul*. The example just cited from counseling with Tim Lyon also illustrates another set of signals of the ending phase of counseling, that of increased clarity concerning the deep issues in the life of the soul. The extended metaphor worked itself through within the framework of Tim's increasingly direct and clear articulation of the issue relative to inflated ambition and experienced failure. He began to lay full claim to this issue as a given for his human existence which had roots deep in his history and the core conflicts of his selfhood. Accepted as a given from which he could not escape, but with which he could continue to struggle with a greater degree of integrity, the issue itself began to give his life a framework of meaning. Clarity about the issue began to shape clarity of purpose and intention which took account of the realities of his life the issue contained.

Not all deep issues of the soul are drawn as sharply as was the issue we have considered from Tim Lyon's life. Neither are all persons as able to articulate the deeper issues of their lives as clearly as was he. Most deep issues of the soul are multifaceted and richly nuanced. It is probably more important, however, that persons come to an end of counseling with some relatively clear conception of the deep issues of their lives as they are than that they be able to articulate all the nuanced ramifications of those issues. Thus a sense of continuing pilgrimage is dependent upon preservation of the sense of "not yet" or incompleteness present in the life of the soul, just as it is dependent upon the awakening of a hopeful possibility for the future. One aspect of this preservation of the sense of being "on the way," rather than of having "arrived," is, of course, a deepened sense of being one with other persons, indeed one with all creation in the condition of "not yet." Clarity concerning the issues that persist in one's own soul breeds clarity concerning the presence of persistent issues in the souls of others.

4. *Signals of openness to transcendence and to the parabolic*. In my earlier book, *Crisis Experience in Modern Life,* I attempted to develop the concept of "incarnational tending to life experience," with a view toward engendering in persons a quality of openness to "signs and symbols of the epiphany of God's disclosure in the events of everyday life."[5] My notion at that time was that if persons are to live their lives with a hermeneutic of hope and expectation in relation to their faith in God's incarnation in the world, a style of openness to life experience was necessary that embodied that faith. The work of chapter 8 suggests that one attribute of an incarnational life-style is a certain parabolic openness—a tendency to interpret the events of everyday life as parables of transcendence. As was said in my earlier discussion, in parabolic interpretation the extraordinary is revealed in the ordinary; transformative possibilities found in the unexpected turn to ordinary narrative experience.

Assuming that one of the things that happens in the course of many successful pastoral counseling relationships is that persons are enabled to appropriate their life experiences as on occasion having parabolic power, one of the signals of the ending phase of counseling may well be an increasing degree of openness to such experiences. Good counseling not only should result in increased self-awareness, but should also open the person to increased awareness of the significance of the flow of events in their lives. The sense of pilgrimage is perhaps best kept alive and active as the flow of events is allowed by the person to speak parabolically. Transformation is process, and process is opened to the transcendent largely in the ways of parable. Signals brought to counseling's ending phase that have the sound of, "such and such happened, and I couldn't help thinking so and so; I found myself wondering what that experience was saying to me," speak of a developing openness to the parabolic. They give us signals that a process has been engendered that has a future beyond the counseling relationship itself.

5. *Signals of appropriation of eschatological identity.* We come now to consider a primary normative criterion for the assessment of the readiness of persons to move ahead with the pilgrimage of their lives upon the completion of a pastoral counseling process: the restoration of persons to some sense of participation in their identity as children of God and heirs of the Kingdom. Within the theological understanding of identity, taken from Jurgen Molt-mann, the way of transcendence into the future of the human pilgrimage is the way of participation in the proleptic possibility of life in the Kingdom within present historical process. Human historical embeddedness cannot be overcome by human power alone, but through our appropriation of eschatological identity we experience the presence and power of the Kingdom in the midst of the ordinariness of historical life. Eschatological identity enables life lived toward the future and open to the lure of that future God is bringing about.

It must be made clear that I am speaking here of something that moves beyond or beneath mere verbal or intellectual assent to the possibility of life in the Kingdom. Appropriation of eschatological identity involves a whole-person response. Indeed, it may or may not involve the use of the language symbols that I have in this book associated with eschatological identity. But the appropriation of eschatological identity does involve the formation of a definable and recognizable stance both toward the self and toward the world in all its relationships. It involves a peculiar stance toward time in all its aspects.

The stance of one who has begun to appropriate his or her eschatological identity will involve the appropriation of a certain attitude toward one's own history and pilgrimage, an attitude perhaps best imaged by the term *acceptance*. One's history is accepted not only as one's own and thereby as unique and necessary to being who one has become, but as setting certain limits and possibilities for the future. The old war against one's history is taken up into some larger acceptance of that history's participation in the history of all things which rests finally on a mystery that can be trusted. The pilgrimage of one's life will have lost some of its loneliness; my pilgrimage has been joined to the pilgrimage of others, indeed of all that is other to the self. As the popular expression puts it, the self will have "joined the human race," no longer seeing itself and its struggles as unique or an exception. The self's pilgrimage, while uniquely and irrevocably personal, is joined with that larger pilgrimage of all persons, all aspects of existence.

This level of acceptance of eschatological identity is often signaled by a reduction in the self's preoccupation with itself and a concomitant enhancement in the self's capacity for concern for and participation with other persons. In the reappropriation and reinterpretation of one's own suffering, a greater sensitivity to the suffering of others has been engendered. The weakness of one's own historical embeddedness has to a significant degree been turned to the strength of an enlarged capacity to care for the welfare of others in their historical situation. Rather than being depleted by the demands and pressures upon the self that threaten the self's existence, the self is increasingly nourished and fulfilled by engagement with others in activities oriented toward the renewal of life together in the spirit of the Kingdom. "True, he died on the cross in weakness, but he lives by the power of God; and we who share his weakness shall by the power of God live with him in your service" (II Corinthians 13:4 NEB).

Lest the reader develop the impression that my understanding of appropriation of eschatological identity involves a virtually utopian vision of the good outcomes of pastoral counseling, it perhaps is important to state clearly that this is not the case. Paradoxical identity, post counseling, remains paradoxical. Life will continue to have its ups and downs, its times of stress and its times of joy. But for the one who at a deep level has begun to make part of the self's narrative a sense of participation in the story of God's activity in behalf of all created life, even the difficult times will be permeated with a quality best symbolized as hope. In the tension between hope and despair, a quality of hopeful integrity will mark the presence of a new balance in the paradox of identity; historical embeddedness will have become balanced by an openness to the self's future in God and to the self's participation in the sufferings of the "not yet" of all things.

And so the intensity of the pastoral counseling relationship comes to an end. The special relationship between two persons whose horizons of understanding have merged for the purpose of providing a particularity of ministry for the help-seeker returns to the ordinariness of life as fellow pilgrims on the way. The help-seeker returns to the ordinariness of finding nurture and stimulation for the pilgrimage in the everyday relationships of his or her life situation. If the counseling has gone well, the help-seeker will have found in the helper a fellow human being who, by the quality of his or her presence in the counseling relationship and by the steadfast patience of his or her insistence that the issues of the life of the soul can be confronted, has opened the hermeneutics of the self to a new and more lively possibility. If the counseling has gone well, the help-seeker will also have found that by the mystery of the power of the Spirit, there are myriad ways in which the lively possibility of continuation of the journey is set before us. Life in its ordinariness, its historical embeddedness, has begun to reveal the extraordinary possibility God has promised.

For the pastoral counselor the ending of a counseling relationship brings both the satisfaction of having entered into the life of the soul of another with helpful purpose and perhaps the humbling recognition that not all one may have hoped for has been accomplished. For the counselor there may remain also the recognition that, in helping, one has been helped; that in the fusion of horizons with another, one's own horizon has been stretched. For the counselor there is also a sense of gratitude to the Spiritual Presence by whose power whatever change that was accomplished was made possible. Sustained by that grateful awareness, the counselor may turn to the next help-seeker with renewed hope and expectation.

E P I L O G U E

Having begun this book with a look at the recent history of pastoral counseling, both in terms of the issues in the literature of the field, and in terms of the story of my own quest for an adequate theory for counseling ministry, it seems appropriate to end the book with a look at the future. The story of pastoral care and counseling is an open-ended story. Like the issues in the life of the soul, the issues of the field are both persistent and ever changing. It is important, therefore, that a book such as this one be seen not as an effort at closure of the continuing dialogue concerning issues in the field, but as pointing a possible direction for future development and discussion.

My afterthoughts cluster around five sets of issues, each of which provides an agenda for further work, not only for me, but for others who may come to these issues with a somewhat different history and perspective. This being an epilogue, it is not my intention to develop these issues fully here, but rather simply to open them and invite the attention of my readers to them as matters that deserve further attention. That being my intention, let us put them in the form of questions calling for further study.

1. Given the psychoanalytic object relations theoretical base upon which the hermeneutical theory has been built from the side of psychology, just what precisely is the relationship between personality dynamics and narrative patterns of meaning in both intrapsychic and interpersonal life?

This is, of course, a restatement of the issue that Paul Ricoeur puts in the language of force and meaning. Which is more basic to the self in determining behavior and relational patterning: force or meaning, personality dynamics or patterns of meaning and symbolic signification? In this book I have pointed to these processes as interlocking and used on occasion the formulation, "force/meaning dynamics" to indicate that these two sides of psychological functioning are so intertwined as to be locked together though perhaps separable. But just how are they interlocked?

Readers probably have sensed in earlier pages a relatively heavier emphasis on the meaning side of the force/meaning equation. At present I would see this imbalance as, in the first instance, a matter of emphasis because of my intention to provide a corrective for pastoral counseling's recent overweening preoccupation with dynamic modes of thinking and language. To emphasize the hermeneutical, symbolic, imagistic side of the equation provides a more readily available avenue of dialogue with theology, most particularly theology's recently renewed interest in narrative.

At another level, however, the emphasis on patterns of symbolic meaning and narrative interpretation represents the manner in which the dynamic force conflicts of the self/ego are most often presented to the pastoral counselor in the clinical context. This is the case not only because the pastor as counselor is seen by persons seeking help as concerned with matters of meaning, symbol, and life story, but also because dynamic conflicts naturally appear in these forms. Just as Freud said of the instinctual drives, dynamic conflicts become visible only in their "representations." Insight into their presence is possible only through the process of interpretation. Furthermore, change in the functioning of ego dynamics involves less the experiencing of them "in the raw," so to speak, than the recognition of their presence relationally through interpretation. In that regard, the psychological language by which these dynamics may be analyzed and interpreted is less useful to the one seeking help than is the everyday language of ordinary speech. In the day-to-day work of pastoral counseling, therefore, the pastor is well advised on a number of counts to work largely within the arena of images, symbols, characterizations, and narrative expression of life conflicts of both force and meaning, dynamic conflict and self efforts of persons to interpret their own experience.

But the issue remains as to just how forces in the self and its environment are related to meanings and symbolic images, or even the extent to which force language is appplicable at all to psychology. This is an anthropological issue that should not simply be left to the psychologists; it is an issue in which both church and ministry have an important stake.

2. Is pastoral counseling in the hermeneutical mode best seen as a form of what traditionally has been called spiritual direction, or is it best imaged as a theologically oriented form of psychotherapy?

This is a multifaceted issue with both practical and theoretical implications. Certainly, when the theoretical framework that is to shape the stance of the pastoral counselor is taken strongly in a self-consciously theological direction, as I have attempted to do in this book, the possibility is opened for a merger of counseling concerning life problems and counseling in matters of the spirit. As a matter of fact, one of the arguments in favor of the theory here proposed is that concern for problems of living and concern for the spiritual life have become too separated in a psychological culture. Ways need to be found for the language of life and the language of the spirit to be restored to a greater unity.

The tradition of spiritual direction has tended in the modern world to be more and more associated with certain forms of esoteric religious language and discipline. This is the case despite, as well as because of, the efforts of such psychologically astute students of spiritual direction as, for example, Henri J. M. Nouwen.[1] Its foundational relationship to religious mysticism and private devotional ritual has been utilized to create an aura of otherworldliness or withdrawal from the mundane affairs of everyday relationships concerning the disciplined life of the spirit.

Against that background of the psychologizing of everyday concern with problems of living and spiritualizing of religious life and devotion, the model of pastoral counseling here proposed may be seen as an alternative lying somewhere midway between pschotherapy and spiritual direction. Fundamentally concerned with the self's pilgrimage through the problems and crises of everyday relational life, the hermeneutical theory is simultaneously concerned with the formation of that side of the self's paradoxical identity rooted and grounded in God and the inbreaking of the kingdom. Here, of course, the theory becomes openly and unashamedly confessional. Insofar as the horizon of understanding brought by the counselor to the counseling relationship is thus involved in confessional faith, to that extent it entails a form of spiritual direction. But insofar as that horizon represents psychological ways of attending to the inner and relational workings of the self, it is a clearly recognizable form of psychotherapy. Partaking of both, the model, both in design and intention, embraces a psycho-spiritual form of ministry.

Here lie a host of theoretical and practical issues relative to the interdisciplinary basis upon which pastoral counseling is to be done, not only by the pastoral counseling specialist, but by the parish pastor whose larger agenda for ministry has to do with moral and spiritual leadership for a community of persons identified as a Christian community. These issues invite further reflection and intellectual analysis by practitioners and pastoral counseling theoreticians alike. It may well turn out to be the case that pastoral counselors have as much to learn from the classical literature of spiritual formation and direction as we have from the modern literature of psychoanalysis and psychotherapy.

3. What of the question concerning long-term versus short-term, problem-oriented pastoral counseling?

Many parish pastors and others who have read through the methodological chapters of this book, with their detailing of such concepts as the fusion of horizons of understanding, the pastoral counseling hermeneutical circle, and the like, may well have wondered with a sigh how they could possibly devote the time and attention to a single individual that these notions presupposed. Likewise, some may have been searching for a more problem-oriented structure for counseling that would focus on the solution to practical relationship problems, the relief of situational or crisis stress, and the early return of persons to less time-consuming and more readily available ways of getting their needs met.

In the explication of the theory, I have maintained throughout that its basic constructs have applicability to both shorter and longer intensive pastoral encounters. It seemed essential on several counts to develop the theory assuming a pastoral counseling relationship over time. Not only do many counseling relationships engaged in by pastoral counseling specialists become extended, but parish pastors, particularly those with extended tenure in the same parish, may have pastoral relationships that extend over a number of years. These relationships may become intensely focused at certain times, followed by periods of occasional serious conversation coupled with the week-to-week encounter in worship or other activities of the church. In either situation shorter-term relationships may well be seen as initiating or facilitating a life process that can be expected to continue more or less indefinitely.

Another presuppositional basis for developing the model in its extended form has to do with the judgment that situational problems, be they problems of marriage and family life, vocation or situational stress such as illness or bereavement, are best understood and best resolved in relation to total life process, the whole of life story. The integration of the self in all its aspects requires that problem solving become integral to the resolution of the total life problem or, in the language of the earlier work, to the work of resolution of the deep issues in the life of the soul. Those issues surface in relation to all kinds of situational problems and become available for intensified effort at finding creative resolution during times of situational or "problem" stress. The ministry of the care of souls demands that effort be made to assist persons in connecting the events and relationships of their lives to these deeper issues of the soul and to the good news of the soul's life in God. Ministry to persons means, among other things, helping them to see their lives as other than an atomistic series of events and problems, each to be encountered as if it were separable from the flow of a life at its deepest and most ultimate levels.

Yet the question remains for further study: Can this hermeneutical theory of pastoral counseling adequately inform ministry in such immediate and apparently short-term problem situations as a life-threatening illness, a bereavement, a threatened divorce, or a family conflict? With modifications to adapt to altered time boundaries, variation in need and purpose on the part of the help-seeker, and comparable modifications to fit the limits and priorities of the pastoral counselor, I believe that it can to a large extent, though not without some important changes in aim, methods, and outcome. The issue, however, merits further work at both practical and theoretical levels.

4. Can a hermeneutical approach to a theory of pastoral *counseling* provide a comparable basis for a theory of pastoral *care* in the parish? What, if any, are the implications then of a hermeneutical theory for a general theory of ministry?

Traditionally the differentiation between pastoral care and pastoral counseling has been made around the question of the presence or absence of a focused problem of relationships or life choice with which the person comes to the pastor seeking help. Seward Hiltner, in his classic 1940s text, *Pastoral Counseling*, uses the term "pre-counseling" for much of the pastor's personal work with those who do not yet have a focused problem toward which counseling as such can be directed.[2] The term "pastoral care" has generally been used to designate that function of the pastor in his or her day-to-day contacts with persons and families relative to the ordinary events of their lives. Birth, death, marriage, times of transition and decision, and so on, provide a loose structure of need and expectation which sets the agenda for pastoral care ministry. The pastor's symbolic role as chief representative of the care of the Christian community provides the authorization for the pastor's active availability to persons in the day-to-day flow of events of their lives.

In practice one of the risks of such a general image of care in pastoral work is that the pastor may become simply a bearer of soft words of concern and support whose general intention to care does not become particularlized. A connection is not made between the pastor's desire to care and the deeper issues in the lives of persons that are shaping the experience of the events that prompt the pastor to be caring.

Here the hermeneutical theory, if utilized as a general theory for understanding the narrative structuring of events and behavior in the lives of persons, provides the pastor with a structure for listening and responding to persons, in ways that care for them at deeper levels of significance. Pastors may not "counsel" with all their parishioners, but they may respond to them in ways that invite attention to the deeper meanings of events and relationships. Thus pastoral care as the care of souls is given both greater specificity and depth. Over time such pastoral conversations with persons, though they never reach the level of intensity of a counseling relationship, may, when coupled with the impact of the pastor's interpretation of the Christian faith from the pulpit and in other contexts, have an impact on the life of the persons' souls of comparable significance.

Beyond the possibility for undergirding pastoral care in the ordinary human situations of parish life, hermeneutical theory offers some potentially fruitful implications for a more general theory of ministry. Ministry theory, like the life of the self, needs more than anything else to become integrated in a wholistic sense. A hermeneutical approach can, I believe, provide an important vehicle for achieving such a unity among pastoral care, preaching, worship and the sacraments, and the educational and group life of the church, and its missional outreach. Seeing ministry in and to the congregation as the tending in all of its aspects of the hermeneutical, interpretive life of a community of persons with a common narrative meaning structure opens interesting and useful ways of envisioning the role of the pastor. The hermeneutical theory in its larger implications concerning the connections between the life of the self and the life of a sociocultural context further suggests ways in which pastoral and social prophetic ministries are mutually connected. Ministry in the community at the social-structural level and ministry to individuals are given greater unity.

All these potential implications of the hermeneutical theory for a more general theory of ministry invite further explication and critical dialogue with other perspectives on ministry theory. Pastoral counseling cannot in and of itself provide an adequate structure for all of ministry. The hermeneutical perspective does, however, provide a basis for further exploration that may lead to an enlarged sense of unity of purpose in ministry practice.

5. When viewed from the more academic standpoint of interdisciplinary studies in theology and personality, has our study suggested a model with broader implications than simply a theory of pastoral counseling?

From the beginning of my work in this book I recognized that the necessity of pastoral counseling's interdisciplinary theoretical base presented me with the problem of the intermingling of language worlds. Not only are the paradigmatic images and core visions of truth about the way things are in the world very different, even disparate, but also each language world is a world in process of change and adaptation to new knowledge. Across such chasms of difference the practitioner of pastoral counseling must find some means of moving back and forth between the disciplines without collapsing one into the other or violating the basic integrity of either.

By its careful and critical attention to the emerging process of psychological theory formulation, pastoral counseling opens itself to the continually shifting horizon of understanding of these more scientific and descriptive ways of viewing human behavior and relationships. Pastoral counseling thus provides theology a window to the world of expanding secular knowledge about the human condition. On the other hand, pastoral counseling contributes a perspective to ongoing discourse concerning psychotherapy in that, if seen as I have here presented it, pastoral counseling argues effectively for the value, even necessity, of placing the process of transformation of self and object relations within a larger context of meaning such as that of a community of faith. Secular psychotherapy, whether performed by a psychologist or a so-called pastoral psychotherapist, by its lack of attention to these larger communal faith and value considerations, is left subject in its outcomes to being simply a tool of the status quo of the sociocultural context in which it takes place. In the world of psychotherapy, pastoral counseling asserts the normative value of Christian images of what human life under God was meant to become. Pastoral counseling is thus not only an important window to the world for theology, but also one of theology's best forms of Christian witness.

Much work remains to be done in the further development of a hermeneutical approach to the interactive process between the disciplines of theology and psychology. Each is developed with a very different set of mythic images of the human self and of the world at its core. In that sense, each provides for the other an antimyth. But, if each is rubbed against the other with care and respect, each may also provide something of parabolic power for the other in that a new and more unifying possibility is opened.

The hermeneutical process continues. Its final outcome is in the hands of him who is the Power of the future. His promise is trustworthy—however problematic it may seem in our present gropings.

Introduction

1. L. Philip Rieff, *The Triumph of the Therapeutic* (New York: Harper & Row, 1966).
2. For an excellent analysis of the interplay of various theological, psychological, and other sociocultural themes in the writings of pastoral care and counseling during this period, see E. Brooks Holifield, *A History of Pastoral Care in America* (Nashville: Abingdon Press, 1983).
3. Seward Hiltner, *Pastoral Counseling* (Nashville/New York: Abingdon-Cokesbury Press, 1949; reprinted 1981).
4. Seward Hiltner, *Preface to Pastoral Theology* (Nashville: Abingdon Press, 1958).
5. Wayne Oates, *Christ and Selfhood* (New York: Association Press, 1961); *Protestant Pastoral Counseling* (Philadelphia: Westminster Press. 1962).
6. Wayne Oates, *Pastoral Counseling* (Philadelphia: Westminster Press, 1974), p. 77.
7. Carroll A. Wise, *Pastoral Counseling: Its Theory and Practice* (New York: Harper and Brothers, 1951); Paul E. Johnson, *The Psychology of Pastoral Care* (Nashville/New York: Abingdon-Cokesbury Press, 1953).
8. Carroll A. Wise, *Pastoral Psychotherapy* (New York: Jason Aronson, 1980).
9. Ibid. pp. 3, 4.
10. Ibid. pp. 25, 26.
11. Howard Clinebell, *Basic Types of Pastoral Counseling* (Nashville: Abingdon Press, 1966).
12. Cf. his *Kerygma and Counseling* (Philadelphia: Westminster Press, 1966); *Contemporary Theology and Psychotherapy* (Westminster Press, 1967); and his *Structures of Awareness* (Nashville: Abingdon Press, 1969).
13. Thomas C. Oden, "Recovering Lost Identity," *The Journal of Pastoral Care*, 345, no. 1 (March 1980):15.
14. In another writing of Thomas Oden, *Agenda for Theology* (San Francisco: Harper & Row, 1979) he so strongly states his disenchantment with twentieth-century consciousness, post Freud, post Marx, post the rise of psychological ways of thinking, as to seem to advocate simply a return to the Christian orthodoxy of the early centuries of the Christian era. His statement in the "Recovering Lost Identity" article I have quoted seems to me both more temperate and more realistic to our current situation.
15. Readers interested in delving into the history of hermeneutics as a philosophical interpretive theory would do well to consult first one of the texts

that trace that history through some of its many permutations since the term was first introduced in ancient times. I have found two such texts particularly helpful: Richard E. Palmer, *Hermeneutics* (Evanston: Northwestern University Press, 1969); and Zygmunt Bauman, *Hermeneutics and Social Science* (New York: Columbia University Press, 1978).

16. Palmer, *Hermeneutics,* p. 13.

1. Life Story and the Story of an Emerging Theory

1. Oliver Spurgeon English and Gerald H. J. Pearson, *Emotional Problems of Living: Avoiding the Neurotic Pattern* (New York: W. W. Norton, 1945).
2. Otto Fenichel, *The Psychoanalytic Theory of Neurosis* (New York: W. W. Norton, 1945).
3. Carl R. Rogers, *On Becoming a Person* (Boston: Houghton Mifflin Co., 1961)
4. Erich Fromm, *Man for Himself* (New York: Rinehart and Co., 1947).
5. Herbert Fingarette, *The Self in Transformation* (New York: Harper & Row, 1965).
6. Philip Rieff, *The Triumph of the Therapeutic* (New York: Harper & Row, 1966).
7. Erich Fromm, *The Heart of Man: Its Genius for Good and Evil* (New York: Harper & Row, 1964).

2. The Living Human Document: Boisen's Image as Paradigm

1. Just when Boisen first used this phrase, which has become legendary in the memory of those who claim him as a professional ancestor, is not certain. He used the term "human document" in print as early as 1930 in an article published in March of that year in *Religious Education.* My own most vivid recollection is of hearing him use the phrase at a Silver Anniversary celebration of the beginnings of clinical pastoral education in Chicago in 1950. That address was later published in *The Journal of Pastoral Care,* vol. 9, no. 1. Boisen then said, "We are trying to call attention back to the central task of the Church, that of 'saving souls,' and to the central problem of theology, that of sin and salvation. *What is new is the attempt to begin with the study of living human documents rather than with books and to focus attention upon those who are grappling desperately with the issues of spiritual life and death.*"
2. Anton Boisen, *The Exploration of the Inner World* (New York: Harper Torchbooks, 1952), p. 11.
3. Ibid., p. 10.
4. For the image of the broken connection I am indebted to Robert Jay Lifton, who, in his book by that title—*The Broken Connection* (New York: Simon and Schuster, 1979)—speaks of a general condition of the mental life of Western culture in which the connection between lived experience and the images and modes by which historically we in the West have organized and given meaning to that experience has been broken. The concern expressed in that image is shared with a number of persons in and near the pastoral counseling field itself. Cf. Paul W. Pruyser, *The Minister as Diagnostician* (Philadelphia: Westminster Press, 1976) and Don S. Browning, *The Moral Context of Pastoral Care* (Philadelphia: Westminster Press, 1976).
5. F. D. E. Schleiermacher, *Hermeneutics: The Handwritten Fragments*, ed. Heinz Kimmerle, trans. James Duke and Jack Forstman (Missoula, Mont.: Scholars Press, 1977), pp. 3-5.

6. Richard E. Palmer, *Hermeneutics* (Evanston: Northwestern University Press, 1969), p.98.
7. Ibid., p. 115.
8. Ibid., p. 116.
9. Ibid., p. 117.
10. Hans-Georg Gadamer, *Truth and Method* (New York: Seabury Press, 1975), pp. 269-74.
11. Ibid., p. 238.
12. Jerome Frank, *Persuasion and Healing*, rev. ed. (New York: Schocken Books, 1974).
13. Hans-Georg Gadamer, *Philosophical Hermeneutics*, trans. and ed. David L. Linge (Berkeley: University of California Press, 1976), pp. 56-57.
14. Boisen, *The Exploration of the Inner World*, p. 11.
15. Paul Tillich, *Systematic Theology*, I (Chicago: University of Chicago Press, 1951), pp. 182-83.
16. Paul Ricoeur, *Freud and Philosophy: An Essay on Interpretation* (New Haven: Yale University Press, 1970).
17. Charles E. Reagan and David Stewart, ed., *The Philosophy of Paul Ricoeur* (Boston: Beacon Press, 1978), p. 169.
18. Paul Ricoeur, *The Conflict of Interpretations: Essays in Hermeneutics*, ed. Don Ihde (Evanston: Northwestern University Press, 1974), pp. 108-9.
19. Herbert Fingarette, *The Self in Transformation: Psychoanalysis, Philosophy, and the Life of the Spirit* (New York: Harper Torchbooks, 1963), pp. 18-29.
20. Ibid., p. 20.

3. Pilgrimage, Incarnation, and the Hermeneutics of the Self

1. Carroll A. Wise, *The Meaning of Pastoral Care* (New York: Harper & Row, 1966), p. 8.
2. James D. Whitehead and Evelyn E. Whitehead, *Method in Ministry* (New York: Seabury Press, 1980), p. 39.
3. James M. Gustafson, "The Relation of the Gospels to the Moral Life," in D. G. Miller and D. Y. Hadidian, ed., *Jesus and Man's Hope* (Pittsburgh: Pittsburgh Theological Seminary, 1971), p. 111.
4. Abraham Heschel, *God in Search of Man* (New York: Farrar, Straus & Giroux, 1955), p. 74.
5. Ibid., pp. 74-75.
6. Ibid., p. 104.
7. Charles V. Gerkin, *Crisis Experience in Modern Life* (Nashville: Abingdon, 1979).
8. R. J. Neuhaus, "Profile of a Theologian," in Wolfhart Pannenberg, *Theology and the Kingdom of God* (Philadelphia: Westminster Press, 1969), p. 46.
9. Paul Tillich, *Systematic Theology*, III (Chicago: University of Chicago Press, 1963), p. 268.
10. Ibid., p. 270.
11. Ibid., p. 276.
12. Ibid., p. 277.
13. Ibid., p. 276.
14. Jurgen Moltmann, *The Trinity and the Kingdom* (San Francisco: Harper & Row, 1981), p. 39.
15. Ibid., p. 19.
16. Ibid.

17. Jurgen Moltmann, *The Crucified God* (New York: Harper & Row, 1974), p. 243.

18. Jurgen Moltmann, *The Church in the Power of the Spirit* (New York: Harper & Row, 1977), p. 191.

19. Ibid., p. 22.

20. Ibid., p. 192.

21. Ibid., p. 193.

22. Jurgen Moltmann, *The Trinity and the Kingdom*, p. 217.

23. Ibid., p. 216.

24. Ibid., p. 125.

25. Jurgen Moltmann, *The Church in the Power of the Spirit*, p. 198.

26. Charles V. Gerkin, *Crisis Experience in Modern Life,* pp. 36, 37.

27. In my earlier book, *Crisis Experience in Modern Life*, this aspect of the pastoral task was termed the engendering of a style of "incarnational tending" to life experience. The concept of pastoral counseling as art of recognition may be seen as an extension of that earlier concept. See *Crisis Experience in Modern Life*, pp. 320, 321.

4. Ego Psychology, Object Relations Theory, and the Hermeneutics of the Self

1. In labeling Freud's vision as a tragicomic one, I am in agreement with such critiques of Freud as that of Philip Rieff (*Freud: The Mind of the Moralist* [Garden City: Doubleday Anchor Books, 1961], pp. 67, 68). Freud saw the human individual as seriously flawed by the vicissitudes of the instincts, but in his emphasis on the possibility of what Rieff calls the "control and manipulation of everyday life" a more optimistic expectation tempered an otherwise somber portrait of human possibility.

2. Anna Freud, *The Ego and the Mechanisms of Defense* (New York: International Universities Press, 1958), p. 178.

3. Heinz Hartmann, *Ego Psychology and the Problem of Adaptation* (New York: International Universities Press, 1958), pp. 8, 9, 10.

4. As was the case with our brief excursion into classical Freudian thought, it would be far beyond the scope and purpose of this book to attempt a thorough summary of object-relations theory. Readers will find in the bibliography a number of primary as well as secondary sources that provide access to some of the key figures in this by now well-developed body of literature. Controversies abound, with a number of schools emphasizing one approach or another to the resolution of the numerous questions that remain unsettled. Perhaps the paramount controversy, interestingly enough, is whether or not Freud's seminal construct of the conflict of the instinctual drives as the primordial given in the formation of the self is to be retained or replaced with a more environmentally oriented or autonomous notion. For purposes of this writing, even that controversial issue may be left to be resolved in the course of future developments in the field.

5. D. W. Winnicott, *The Maturational Processes and the Facilitating Environment* (London: Hogarth Press, 1965), p. 46.

6. Ibid., p. 61.

7. Ibid., p. 57.

8. Madelaine Davis and David Wallbridge, *Boundary and Space: An Introduction to the Work of D. W. Winnicott* (New York: Brunner/Mazel, Publishers, 1981), pp. 40, 41.

9. D. W. Winnicott, *Playing and Reality* (New York: Basic Books, 1971), p. 2.
10. Anna-Maria Rizzuto, *The Birth of the Living God* (Chicago: University of Chicago Press, 1979).
11. Winnicott, *The Maturational Processes and the Facilitating Environment*, p. 145.
12. In my own appropriation of Otto Kernberg's theoretical work, I have been greatly assisted by discussions with my colleague at Emory University, Charles D. Hackett, whose unpublished, privately circulated paper, "Psychoanalysis and Theology: Two Dialectics," presents a careful analysis of Kernberg's work. I have also drawn primary source material from Otto Kernberg, *Object Relations Theory and Clinical Psychoanalysis* (New York: Jason Aronson, 1976).
13. Kernberg, *Object Relations Theory*, p. 40.
14. Heinz Kohut, *The Restoration of the Self* (New York: International Universities Press, 1977), p. 132.
15. Ibid., p. 271.
16. Ibid., p. 133.
17. Ibid., p. 180.
18. Ibid., p. 182.
19. Ibid., pp. 177, 178.
20. See especially Erik H. Erikson, *Childhood and Society* (New York: W. W. Norton, 1950); *Insight and Responsibility* (New York: W. W. Norton, 1964); and Erik H. Erikson, editor, *Adulthood* (New York: W. W. Norton, 1976).

5. The Hermeneutics of the Self and the Life of the Soul

1. Readers are again referred here to the works by Erikson cited in chapter 4.
2. Cf. James W. Fowler, *Stages of Faith* (New York: Harper & Row, 1981).
3. Though Erikson's work is foundational here, we would also include the more recent work of others, particularly on the stages of adult life. Cf. Daniel J. Levinson, *The Seasons of a Man's Life* (New York: Alfred a. Knopf, 1978). Unfortunately, Levinson's work is based only on his observations with a sampling of middle-and upper-class males and thereby develops less than half the full adult human picture. The popularization of stage theories of adulthood by such authors as Gail Sheehy *(Passages: Predictable Crises of Adult Life* [New York: E. P. Dutton, 1974]) and Roger Gould *(Transformations: Growth and Change in Adult Life* [New York: Simon and Schuster, 1978]) has so influenced the language of popular culture concerning adult experience at the level of life cycle time as to create a cliché regarding the so-called mid-life crisis.
4. Jurgen Moltmann, *The Church in the Power of the Spirit* (New York: Harper & Row, 1977), p. 192.
5. Stanley Hauerwas, "Story and Theology," *Religion and Life*, Autumn, 1976, p. 344.
6. Wesley A. Kort, *Narrative Elements and Religious Meaning* (Philadelphia: Fortress Press, 1975), p. 18.
7. Ibid., p. 35.
8. Ibid., p. 91.

6. Evoking the Story in the Stories of the Self

1. Readers who wish to pursue the problem of unraveling the layers of interpretation in a psychotherapeutic relationship would do well to consult a

growing body of psychoanalytic literature dealing with the problem. I have myself found two readings particularly useful in this regard: Donald P. Spence, *Narrative Truth and Historical Truth: Meaning and Interpretation in Psychoanalysis* (New York: W. W. Norton, 1982); and Serge Viderman, "The Analytic Space: Meaning and Problems," *Psychoanalytic Quarterly,* 1979. Spence persuasively argues that even such standard psychoanalytic procedures as free association on the part of the analysand and free-floating attention on the part of the analyst are made problematic by the pervasive presence of interpretive language.

2. Zygmunt Bauman, *Hermeneutics and Social Science* (New York: Columbia University Press, 1978), p.17.

7. Changing the Story: Psychoanalytic, Hermeneutical, and Theological Perspectives

1. For a well balanced theological/ethical appraisal of behavior modification techniques of behavioral change, the reader is referred to Clyde J. Steckel, *Theology and Ethics of Behavior Modification* (Washington, D.C.: University Press of America, 1979).

2. Otto Kernberg, *Object Relations Theory and Clinical Psychoanalysis* (New York: Jason Aronson, 1976), p. 121.

3. Paul Ricoeur, *Hermeneutics and the Social Sciences* (Cambridge: Cambridge University Press, 1981), pp. 11, 12.

4. For a relatively nontechnical description of the phenomenon of transference in psychotherapy and its careful monitoring by the therapist to effect change brought about by regression in the transference, see Karl Menninger and Philip S. Holzman, *Theory of Psychoanalytic Technique,* 2nd ed. (New York: Basic Books, 1973).

5. Much more could, of course, be said here concerning both the need of pastoral counselors for the experience of counseling under supervision that attends to the interplay of personal and professional learning and the need of pastoral counselors for consultation. Standards for both the certification of pastoral counselors and the practice of the discipline maintained by such organizations as the American Association of Pastoral Counselors provide excellent guidelines in these matters. While I generally support these guild efforts to create standards of excellence for pastoral counseling as a discipline among the helping professions, the orientation of the theory being developed in this book would enfold pastoral counseling more closely into the life and language of the church than many practitioners in A.A.P.C. now evidence in their practice. The theory is intended as a framework for both counseling done by the parish pastor who takes his or her counseling ministry seriously and counseling done by the pastoral counseling specialist.

6. For a more detailed explication of the strands of pastoral theological tradition relative to the pastoral care relationship, cf. my *Crisis Experience in Modern Life,* pp. 36, 37, 38.

8. Changing the Story: Myth and Parable in Pastoral Counseling

1. John Dominic Crossan, *The Dark Interval: Towards a Theology of Story* (Allen, Texas: Argus Communications, 1975), p. 59.

2. Ibid., pp. 59, 60.

3. "But these relationships are not to world *outside* story, world which story describes and imitates, but to world *inside* story, world which story creates and defines" (ibid.).

4. In the opening chapter of John Dominic Crossan's book from which I have taken the typology of the ways of language in story, Crossan, drawing from a number of philosophers and literary figures who have considered the problem of pluralism of language worlds, provides his readers with an excellent and highly readable introduction to this problem. Readers who for various reasons are not interested in engaging in an in-depth exploration of the philosophical literature on this complex problem of epistemology will find in Crossan's chapter a sound, if simple, summary of the issues involved.

5. For an excellent psychotherapeutic theory concerning marriage contracts, see Clifford J. Sager, *Marriage Contracts and Couple Therapy* (New York: Brunner/Mazel Publishers, 1976).

6. John Dominic Crossan, *The Dark Interval*, p. 60.

7. Sallie McFague, *Speaking in Parables* (Philadelphia: Fortress Press, 1975), p. 79.

8. *Crisis Experience in Modern Life*, pp. 196-201.

9. John Dominic Crossan, *In Parables: The Challenge of the Historical Jesus* (New York: Harper & Row, 1973), p. 35.

10. Ibid., p. 36.

11. McFague, *Speaking in Parables*, p. 45.

12. Crossan, *In Parables*, p. 84.

13. Erik Erikson, *The Life Cycle Completed* (New York: W. W. Norton, 1982), p. 73. Since I have made reference to Erik Erikson's schema of psychosocial developmental dilemmas, it is important to take note of the manner in which Tim Lyon's repudiation of his "fast lane" ambitions represented a long delayed resolution of an earlier developmental dilemma more commonly resolved during adolescence. Having prematurely been pressed from early in his life into stage inappropriate adult responsibility for his parents, Tim had been unable to fulfill the normal adolescent task of identity formation involving what Erikson speaks of as developing fidelity to assumed roles and repudiation of roles and values not chosen. Now in the middle years of his life, Tim was having to work through the critical dilemmas of a much earlier life cycle stage.

14. Crossan, *The Dark Interval*, pp. 124, 125.

9. The Ending Phase:
Pastoral Counseling and the
Community of the Christian Story

1. Cf. William B. Oglesby, *Referral in Pastoral Counseling* (Nashville: Abingdon, 1978).

2. Although I will have more to say concerning the applicability of our hermeneutical perspective to the structuring of a general ministry of pastoral care in the life of the community of faith in the Epilogue, limits of space and purpose for this book prevent full development of the implications of the theory for a general theory of pastoral care. That is work yet to be undertaken. The possibilities, for example, of developing a theory of pastoral ministry utilizing the structure of John Dominic Crossan's typology of the five ways of language in story are indeed promising, having applicability to consideration of such questions as the relationship of worship and liturgy, as well as preaching, to pastoral care in the corporate community context.

3. Jurgen Moltmann, *The Church in the Power of the Spirit*, pp. 21, 22.

4. Jurgen Moltmann, with M. Douglas Meeks, Rodney J. Hunter, James W. Fowler, and Noel L. Erskine, *Hope for the Church: Moltmann in Dialogue with Practical Theology* (Nashville: Abingdon, 1979), pp. 91, 92.
5. *Crisis Experience in Modern Life*, pp. 320, 321, 322.

Epilogue

1. Henri J. M. Nouwen, *The Living Reminder: Service and Prayer in Memory of Jesus Christ* (New York: The Seabury Press, 1977).
2. Seward Hiltner, *Pastoral Counseling* (Nashville: Abingdon, 1949), pp. 128-48.

BIBLIOGRAPHY

Theology

Texts most significant for the theological stance of this book:

Heshel, Abraham Joshua. *God in Search of Man: A Philosophy of Judaism.* New York: Farrar, Straus and Giroux 1955.

Moltmann, Jurgen. *The Church in the Power of the Spirit.* New York: Harper & Row, 1977.

———. *The Trinity and the Kingdom.* New York: Harper & Row, 1981.

Niebuhr, H. Richard. *The Responsible Self: An Essay in Moral Philosophy.* New York: Harper & Row, 1963.

Pannenberg, Wolfhart. *Theology and the Kingdom of God.* Philadelphia: Westminster Press, l969.

Tillich, Paul. *Systematic Theology,* vol. III. Chicago: University of Chicago Press, 1963.

Other important books by the same theologians:

Heschel, Abraham Joshua. *Man's Quest for God: Studies in Prayer and Symbolism.* New York: Scribner's 1954.

Moltmann, Jurgen. *Theology of Hope.* New York: Harper & Row, 1967.

———. *The Crucified God.* New York: Harper & Row, 1974.

———. *The Future of Creation.* Philadelphia: Fortress Press, 1979.

———. with Douglas Meeks, Rodney J. Hunter, James W. Fowler, and Noel Erskine. Trans. and ed. Theodore Runyon. *Hope for the Church: Moltmann in Dialogue with Practical Theology.* Nashville: Abingdon, 1979.

———. *Experiences of God.* Philadelphia: Fortress Press, 1980.

Niebuhr, H. Richard. *The Meaning of Revelation.* New York: Macmillan, 1941.

———. *Radical Monotheism and Western Culture.* New York: Harper and Bros., 1943.

Pannenberg, Wolfhart. *What Is Man? Contemporary Anthropology in Theological Perspective*. Philadelphia: Fortress Press, 1970.
Tillich, Paul. *Systematic Theology*, vol. I. Chicago: University of Chicago Press, 1951.
———. *Systematic Theology*, vol. II. Chicago: University of Chicago Press, 1957.

Related books in theology and ethics:

Barfield, Owen. *Saving the Appearances: A Study in Idolatry*. New York: Harcourt, Brace, 1965.
Evans, Robert A., and Parker, Thomas D., *Christian Theology: Case Study Approach*. New York: Harper & Row, 1976.
Gustafson, James M. "The Relation of the Gospels to the Moral Life," in D. G. Miller and D. Y. Hadidian, editors, *Jesus and Man's Hope*. Pittsburgh, Pittsburgh Theological Seminary, 1971.
Hauerwas, Stanley. *Vision and Virtue: Essays in Christian Ethical Reflection*. Notre Dame: Fides Publishers, 1974.
———. *Character and the Christian Life: A Study in Theological Ethics*. San Antonio: Trinity University Press, 1975.
———. *A Community of Character*. Notre Dame: University of Notre Dame Press, 1981.
Hodgson, Peter C. *Jesus—Word and Presence: An Essay in Christology*. Philadelphia: Fortress Press, 1971.
Lynch, William F. *Christ and Apollo*. New York: Mentor-Omega Books, 1963.
———. *Images of Hope: Imagination as Healer of the Hopeless*. Notre Dame, University of Notre Dame Press, 1965.
———. *Images of Faith: An Exploration of the Ironic Imagination*. Notre Dame: University of Notre Dame Press, 1973.
McClendon, James W., Jr. *Biography as Theology: How Life Stories Can Remake Today's Theology*. Nashville: Abingdon Press, 1974.
Metz, Johann Baptist. *Faith in History and Society: Toward a Practical Fundamental Theology*. New York: Seabury Press, 1980.
Nouwen, Henri J. M. *The Wounded Healer*. Garden City, N. Y.: Doubleday, 1972.
———. *The Living Reminder: Service and Prayer in Memory of Jesus Christ*. New York: Seabury Press, 1977.
Oden, Thomas. *Kerygma and Counseling*. Philadelphia: Westminster Press, 1966.
———. *Contemporary Theology and Psychotherapy*. Philadelphia: Westminster Press, 1967.
———. *Structures of Awareness*. Nashville: Abingdon Press, 1969.
———. *Agenda for Theology*. San Francisco: Harper & Row, 1979.
Steckel, Clyde J. *Theology and Ethics of Behavior Modification*. Washington: University Press of America, 1979.
Tracy, David. *Blessed Rage for Order*. New York: Seabury Press, 1975.
———. *The Analogical Imagination*. New York: Seabury Press, 1978.

Pastoral Theology and Pastoral Care

Modern pastoral care classics:

Boisen, Anton. *The Exploration of the Inner World.* New York: Harper Torchbook, 1952.

Hiltner, Seward. *Pastoral Counseling.* Nashville: Abingdon Press, 1949.

———. *Preface to Pastoral Theology.* Nashville: Abingdon Press, 1958.

Oates, Wayne E. *Protestant Pastoral Counseling.* Philadelphia: Westminster Press, 1962.

Williams, Daniel Day. *The Minister and the Care of Souls.* New York: Harper and Bros., 1961.

Wise, Carroll A. *Pastoral Counseling: Its Theory and Practice.* New York: Harper and Bros., 1951.

———. *The Meaning of Pastoral Care.* New York: Harper & Bros., 1966.

Books of recent historical importance:

Clinebell, Howard. *Basic Types of Pastoral Care and Counseling.* Nashville: Abingdon Press, 1966; rev. and enlgd., 1984.

Johnson, Paul E. *Person and Counselor.* Nashville: Abingdon Press, 1967.

Oates, Wayne E. *Christ and Selfhood.* New York: Association Press, 1961.

———. *Pastoral Counseling.* Philadelphia: Westminster Press, 1974.

Recent books of value and interest:

Browning, Don S. *The Moral Context of Pastoral Care.* Philadelphia: Westminster Press, 1976.

Capps, Donald. *Biblical Approaches to Pastoral Counseling.* Philadelphia: Westminster Press, 1981.

Clinebell, Howard. *Basic Types of Pastoral Care and Counseling.* Revised and enlarged edition. Nashville: Abingdon Press, 1984.

Gerkin, Charles V. *Crisis Experience in Modern Life: Theory and Theology for Pastoral Care.* Nashville: Abingdon, 1979.

Holifield, E. Brooks. *A History of Pastoral Care in America.* Nashville: Abingdon Press, 1983.

Oden, Thomas C. "Recovering Lost Identity," in *Journal of Pastoral Care* 34, no. 1 (1980).

———. *Pastoral Theology: Essentials of Ministry.* Harper & Row, 1982.

Oglesby, William B. Jr. *Referral in Pastoral Counseling.* Nashville: Abingdon, 1978.

———. *Biblical Themes for Pastoral Care.* Nashville: Abingdon, 1980.

Pruyser, Paul W. *The Minister as Diagnostician.* Philadelphia: Westminster Press, 1976.

Whitehead, James D., and Whitehead, Evelyn E. *Method in Ministry.* New York: Seabury Press, 1980.

Wimberly, Edward P. *Pastoral Counseling and Spiritual Values: A Black Point of View*. Nashville: Abingdon, 1982.

Hermeneutics

I found all the literature in hermeneutics difficult, but rewarding. Readers should consider beginning with one of the following introductory survey texts:

Bauman, Zygmunt. *Hermeneutics and Social Science*. New York: Columbia University Press, 1978.
Palmer, Richard E. *Hermeneutics*. Evanston: Northwestern University Press, 1969.

Other general surveys:

Bleicher, Josef. *Contemporary Hermeneutics: Hermeneutics as Method, Philosophy and Critique*. London: Routledge and Kegan Paul, 1980.
Braaten, Carl E. *History and Hermeneutics*. *Philadelphia:* Westminster Press, 1966.
Howard, Roy J. *Three Faces of Hermeneutics: An Introduction to Current Theories of Understanding*. Los Angeles: University of California, 1982.

Some major contemporary figures in the field:

Gadamer, Hans-Georg. *Philosophical Hermeneutics*. Berkeley: University of California Press, 1976.
———. *Truth and Method*. New York: Crossroad, 1982.
Habermas, Jurgen. *Knowledge and Human Interests*. Boston: Beacon Press, 1971.
Ihde, Don. *Hermeneutic Phenomenology: The Philosophy of Paul Ricoeur*. Evanston: Northwestern University Press, 1971.
Reagan, Charles E., and Stewart, David, ed. *The Philosophy of Paul Ricoeur*. Boston: Beacon Press, 1978.
Ricoeur, Paul. *Freedom and Nature: The Voluntary and the Involuntary*. Evanston: Northwestern University Press, 1966.
———. *The Symbolism of Evil*. Boston: Beacon Press, 1967.
———. *Freud and Philosophy: An Essay on Interpretation*. New Haven: Yale University Press, 1970.
———. *The Conflict of Interpretations*. Evanston: Northwestern University Press, 1974.
———. *Hermeneutics and the Human Sciences*. Cambridge: Cambridge University Press, 1981.

Related books:

Bacon, Wallace A. *The Art of Interpretation*, 2nd ed. New York: Holt, Rinehart and Winston, 1972.

Kroner, Richard, *The Religious Function of Imagination*. New Haven: Yale University Press, 1941.

Schleiermacher, F. D. E. *Hermeneutics: The Handwritten Fragments*. Ed. Heinz Kimmerle, trans. James Duke and Jack Fortman. Missoula, Mont.: Scholars Press, 1977.

Winquist, Charles E. *Homecoming: Interpretation, Transformation and Individuation*. Chico, Calif.: Scholars Press, 1978.

————. *Practical Hermeneutics: A Revised Agenda for the Ministry*. Chico, Calif.: Scholars Press, 1981.

Parable and Narrative

Books cited in this book:

Crossan, John Dominic. *In Parables*. New York: Harper and Row, 1973.

————. *The Dark Interval: Towards a Theology of Story*. Allen, Texas.: Argus Communications, 1975.

Kort, Wesley A. *Narrative Elements and Religious Meanings*. Philadelphia: Fortress Press, 1975.

McFague, Sallie. *Speaking in Parables: A Study in Metaphor and Theology*. Philadelphia: Fortress Press, 1975.

Other useful books and articles:

Crites, Stephen. "The Narrative Quality of Experience," in *Journal of the American Academy of Religion*, 1971, pp. 290-307.

Niebuhr, Richard R. *Experiential Religion*. New York: Harper & Row, 1972.

Stoneburner, Tony, ed. *Parable, Myth and Language*. Cambridge: Church Society for College Work, 1968.

Wilder, Amon N. *Jesus' Parables and the War of Myths*. James Breech, ed. Philadelphia: Fortress Press, 1982.

Ego Psychology, Object Relations Theory

Classics in ego psychology:

Erikson, Erik H. *Childhood and Society*. New York: W. W. Norton, 1960.

————.*Insight and Responsibility*. New York: W. W. Norton, 1964.

Freud, Anna. *The Ego and the Mechanisms of Defense*. New York: International Universities Press, 1958.

Freud, Sigmund. *The Ego and the Id*. James Strachey, ed. New York: W. W. Norton, 1960.

Hartmann, Heinz. *Ego Psychology and the Problem of Adaptation*. New York: International Universities Press, 1958.

Jacobson, Edith. *The Self and the Object World*. New York: International Universities Press, 1964.

Introductory texts:

Blanck, Gertrude, and Blanck, Rubin. *Ego Pschology I: Theory and Practice.* New York: Columbia University Press, 1975.
————.*Ego Pschology II.* New York: Columbia University Press, 1979.

Object relations theorists cited in this book:

Davis, Madeleine, and Wallbridge, Daniel. *Boundary and Space: An Introduction to the work of D. W. Winnicott.* New York: Brunner/Mazel, 1981.
Kernberg, Otto. *Object Relations Theory and Clinical Psychoanalysis.* New York: Jason Aronson, 1976.
————. *Internal World and External Reality.* New York: Jason Aronson, 1981.
————. *Object Relations Theory and Its Applications.* New York: Jason Aronson, 1981.
Kohut, Heinz. *The Analysis of the Self.* New York: International Universities Press, 1971.
————. *The Restoration of the Self.*New York: International Universities Press, 1977.
Rizzuto, Anna-Maria. *The Birth of the Living God.* Chicago: The University of Chicago Press, 1979.
Winnicott, D. W. *The Maturational Processes and the Facilitating Environment.* London: Hogarth Press, 1965.
————. *Playing and Reality.* New York: Basic Books. 1971.
————. *The Piggle: An Account of the Psychoanalytic Treatment of a Little Girl.* New York: International Universities Press, 1977.

Related books of value:

Erikson, Erik H. *Life History and the Historical Moment.* New York: W. W. Norton, 1971.
————. ed. *Adulthood.* New York: W. W. Norton, 1976.
————. *Toys and Reasons: Stages in the Ritualization of Experience.* New York: W. W. Norton, 1977.
————. *The Life Cycle Completed.* New York: W. W. Norton, 1982.
Fingarette, Herbert. *The Self in Transformation.* New York: Harper & Row, 1965.
Fowler, James A. *Stages of Faith.* New York: Harper & Row, 1981.
Fromm, Erich. *Man for Himself.* New York: Rinehart and Co., 1947.
————. *The Heart of Man: Its Genius For Good and Evil.* New York: Harper & Row, 1964.
Guntrip, Harry. *Psychoanalytic Theory, Therapy, and the Self.* New York: Basic Books, 1971.
Kegan, Robert. *The Evolving Self: Problem and Process in Human Development.* Cambridge: Harvard University Press, 1982.

Levinson, Daniel J. *The Seasons of a Man's Life*. New York: Alfred A. Knopf, 1978.

Lifton, Robert Jay. *The Life of the Self: Toward a New Psychology*. New York: Simon and Schuster, 1976.

————.*The Broken Connection*. New York: Simon and Schuster, 1979.

May, Rollo. *Love and Will*. New York: W. W. Norton, 1969.

————. *Freedom and Destiny*. New York: W. W. Norton, 1981.

Pruyser, Paul W. *The Psychological Examination: A Guide for Clinicians*. New York: International Universities Press, 1979.

Psychoanalysis and Psychotherapy

A selection with particular relevance to this book:

English, O. S., and Pearson, G. H. J. *Emotional Problems of Living: Avoiding the Neurotic Pattern*. New York: W. W. Norton, 1945.

Fenichel, Otto. *The Psychoanalytic Theory of Neurosis*. New York: W. W. Norton, 1945.

Leowald, Hans. W. *Pschoanalysis and the History of the Individual*. New Haven: Yale University Press, 1978.

Menninger, Karl, with Martin Mayman and Paul Pruyser. *The Vital Balance: The Life Process in Mental Illness and Health*. New York: Viking, 1963.

Menninger, Karl, and Holzman, Philip S. *Theory of Psychoanalytic Technique*, 2nd ed. New York: Basic Books, 1973.

Rogers, Carl R. *On Becoming a Person*. Boston: Houghton Mifflin Co., 1961.

Sager, Clifford J. *Marriage Contracts and Couple Therapy*. New York: Brunner/ Mazel Publishers, 1976.

Schafer, Roy. *A New Language for Psychoanalysis*. New Haven: Yale University Press, 1976.

Spence, Donald P. *Narrative Truth and Historical Truth: Meaning and Interpretation in Psychoanalysis*. New York: W. W. Norton, 1982.

Wise, Carrol A. *Pastoral Psychotherapy*. New York: Jason Aronson, 1980.

Psychology and Social Science

A miscellaneous list of varying importance for this book:

Everett, William, W., and Bachmeyer, T. J. *Disciplines in Transformation: A Guide to Theology and the Behavioral Sciences*. Washington: University Press of America, 1979.

Frank, Jerome. *Persuasion and Healing*, rev. ed. New York: Schocken Books, 1974.

Hillman, James. *Re-Visioning Psychology*. New York: Harper & Row, 1975.

Reiff, Philip. *Freud: The Mind of the Moralist*. Garden City, N. Y.: Doubleday Anchor Books, 1961.

————. *The Triumph of the Therapeutic.* New York: Harper & Row, 1966.

Schutz, Alfred, and Luckmann, Thomas. Trans. Richard M. Zaner and H. Tristram Engelhardt, Jr. *The Structures of the Life-World.* Evanston: Northwestern University Press, 1973.